Prof Gerrit Olivier
Rapport: 19 November 2006

"The novel shows another face₋ *oj ₋ₙₑ ₋ₙⱼⱼ₋ ₋*
past under Apartheid. What makes it moving is the manner in
which it places emphasis on human values way above racist
categorization."

Justice Edwin Cameron
Constitutional Court Judge and Author of *Witness to AIDS*

Sunday Independent: Books Page December 2006
'BEST READS OF THE YEAR'

'kaffertjie,' by Johan Engelbrecht is a provocatively titled novel-
ization of a most remarkable true story. The writer's childless aunt
and uncle – he was a West Rand Conservative Party councillor in
the 1980s – took their helper's infant into their doting care when
she became permanently institutionalized. The title is eponymous,
and is meant to capture the contradictions in this story of love,
devotion and (fortunately brief) betrayal across the chasms of racial
ignorance and stupidity. The book is already making waves in its
Afrikaans appearance."

Justice Edwin Cameron
Rapport: 19 November 2006

"This is an important moment in Afrikaans literature. Now is the
time to write honest stories about Apartheid. So many books from
this era are filled with self-pity, but this book doesn't have a trace
of it. It is written with so much insight that it takes you right back
to that time, as well as taking you back to connecting with your
own heart."

1

kaffertjie
a love story

Johan Engelbrecht

Translation by Jocelyn Broderick

Johan Engelbrecht ©
Email: johan@kaffertjie.co.za
www.kaffertjie.com

Translation by Jocelyn Broderick ©
Email: jossiebrod@mweb.co.za

FIRST EDITION October 2011

kaffertjie
(little kaffir boy)

I was born just after the turn of the twentieth century and was already in my early eighties when this thing happened to us.

Even from an early age a woman is modest about things like this. Ageing. We retain that modesty. But now, at my age, I am mostly grateful and rather proud of it. Eighty-two, thank you very much, and blessed with a clear mind.

I believed that in my lifetime I would get used to everything. From ox-wagons to people on the moon. The Beatles. And the mini skirt.

And then came the year of eighty-six. Nothing could have prepared me for it. We came face to face with the last of the Triple Terrors: the Black Terror! "Our country is burning," I heard them say over and over the past year. All I have to say is this: "I saw this thing coming right from the start." There were three Great Terrors: The Commies; the Catholics and now this one. The Blacks! The Terrorists!

We were brought up on a diet of Fear – to fear everything in heaven and on earth – and I spoon-fed it bottle by bottle to the children, and they did so in turn to my grand- and my great grandchildren.

You could get it everywhere. Along with the Terror came the Fear. So we closed our eyes and hearts tightly, and prayed that we would be spared and come out in one piece on the other side.

If you weren't caught in the grips of this fear, it's not so easy to understand. It's hard to see beyond the blinkers put on by those who daily paralyze you with more and more fear.

And the stories. Everyone suddenly had a tale to tell. We pitied the Roman Catholics who would burn in hell because they had strayed off the path, and the Communists were, according to Heinz Konsalik, mostly in Russia, with spies watching their every move. The torture of believers and the banning of the Holy Book were known world-wide. People everywhere were equally terrified of the blackness of the catacombs.

Tonight people all over the world are sleeping with one eye open.

They also wanted to strip us of our freedom and beliefs, both then and now, they tell us. "Our freedom! Our beliefs! They want all our belongings, our homes, our cars. They just want to take-take-take. They want money. They want the right to vote. They want everything!" We get bombarded with this on every corner. And in our sleep we begin to grind our teeth.

And then we are still God-fearing creatures on top of it all!

Selah.

However.

"There are some Commies loose amongst the natives," or whatever we call them at this point in time, "and they are getting restless," you hear whispered around. The hair on the back of the white's necks stands up as straight as a die. And with this hair standing up dead straight, we form a *laager*. That's what we do. We retreat further. We round up the ox-wagons to close everything else out. We overcame them before with a *laager*, a few *Boer* muskets and a covenant. Right there and then we started writing our own history. The thing about a *laager* is that what's inside stays inside. And belongs there. Anything trying to get in from the outside looks like an attack.

Another terror. Heaven protect us. And we take off. We defend. We even start shooting at our own kind. It's because one eventually can't see beyond the circle of ox-wagons.

And then one day it happens right under your nose.

You see it, but you can't recognize it for what it is.

Ester was the second youngest of my daughters and the third youngest of my eight children. Let me tell it as it is: She is my prettiest.

That it happened to her is almost already the answer to the question. The scholars have probably already found a name for it. But a name alone doesn't bring understanding.

I was never schooled, as in my day it wasn't seen as necessary. Or that's what we were told. A woman's place was not what it is today. A woman's place was in the home, along with all the duties that went hand in hand with it. A true woman was one who stood by her man, as she agreed to do in her marriage vows. You did what you had to do.

I was named Susanna Magdalena, after my mother's mother.

I found a good man, Joshua Samuel. Two books of the Bible. A man true to both names. I lost my partner a few years after our Golden Wedding Anniversary. But I was content.

Ester also got herself a good man. We knew him well, ages before he and Ester got married. And that's the reason why their marriage bothered us so much in the beginning.

He was christened Paulus, after the chosen one, and Daniël, the one persecuted because of his faith. We knew him as Paul. Paul de Villiers.

Ah, the relentless Biblical names that hung like a noose around our necks. And with so many children, five daughters and three sons, and this thing with two names each; there was much long and intense paging through the Bible to find some kind of name for those who had missed out on the family names.

Ester Wilhelmina – both such regal names – and Paul live on a smallholding of nearly four hectares in Witpoortjie on the Witwatersrand. They fell into the municipality of Roodepoort, which was called a city within the city of Johannesburg because of the many people living there.

Their smallholding looks like a farm in every way. You have to make your way through the wretched crooked gate, with a lock and chain, along the double tracked gravel road, past the farm dam and windmill, until you reach the face-brick house with its corrugated iron roof.

They "farmed" with six cows for milk, and a few sheep and chickens for meat and eggs. Paul also kept racing pigeons.

The Witwatersrand is heaven on earth for man and beast, but has no patience when it comes to plants. It is the merciless frost that can burn plants pitch-black overnight. It even makes feeding this handful of livestock hard.

The winter is cruel but short.

Paul is a large man who went grey at an early age.

He sports a tamed moustache and short hair. He looks stern but his face is sympathetic. He barks and barks. But his bark is worse than his bite.

He has such bright eyes. So has Ester. Almost light blue when the sun dances in them. He cries easily. He is not ashamed to be seen with traces of tears drying on his cheeks. A refined man. One of the few we know who enjoys classical music. Along with the Minister of our Church and the organist. That stuff could make him cry so easily.

"It's because of its beauty, Mother," and his eyes brim with tears as he listens to the high voices of people who sing in strange languages.

It's a late Sunday-afternoon thing. When the silence descends upon us.

Ester's eyes have a deeply defined dark ring around the iris. On a clear day you feel as if you can see right through her.

She's a redhead.

He's a true gentleman.

He turned Ester into a lady. Never a madam. She has no frills and fancies.

As a child on the farm she rode the calves just like any boy could. The boys caught them so that Ester could have her turn. She could sit tight, sitting tight no matter how high they bucked.

He tamed my wildest child.

We all looked up to him.

The dawn is late and it is still almost dark when Paul picks up the buckets of feed just near the house and starts walking in the direction of the dam. It's winter and every-thing is bleak and leafless. It's beautiful if you can see the beauty, otherwise it is just pale. Sallow. Stripped of colour.

It's golden yellow to me.

He always wears a blue overall and rubber boots at this time of the morning. Underneath he is already dressed complete with tie, pullover and all that goes with it. Ready for the rest of the day. He carries a bucket in each hand. He puts the buckets down at the chicken coop, takes a handful of corn out of a Hessian sack and throws it into the coop. Only a few of them scurry about. The rest are still lying in the feathers feeling the cold. He picks up the buckets and walks on. Yapping and scampering under his feet are a flurry of Toypom dogs.

In his heart of hearts he is a farmer.

For a moment he stands still, watching the wheel of the windmill that screeches while turning slowly. A drop of oil will stop its lament. But how does one then know that the thing is turning? The worry kicks in when it becomes silent.

It can get very dry in this world.

He moves off around the coops and walks into the open veld. Here, against his better judgement, he's tried to plant Lucerne once or twice. But now it's just the grass and the blackened skeletons of the Peach-; Plum- and Apricot trees which will only come to life again in a month or two. The grass this year is almost at knee-height and it crackles under his boots. This is not a path for anyone to walk barefoot.

Emily is on her way to the De Villiers home from the opposite direction. Her and Amos' room is to one side, but still near to the house. She's been here four years. According to Ester she was just a child, around fourteen, when Amos brought her here. He was barely twenty himself when he started with us.

She sings while she walks. She sings softly but her voice can be heard a mile away. She carries a small bundle on her back. It's a little boy.

For me the early morning is a wonderful thing.

I was already on my chair at the window, a nice high one with wooden armrests and a straight back, with my crochet-work on my lap, when the commotion began.

Once I've enjoyed my first cup of coffee I sit in anticipation waiting for the day to begin. Partly from thankfulness, because by then I know that I am still here; and otherwise, because the sunlight makes it easier for me to see the dark wool.

It's Moola's here in Roodepoort's fault. The Bottle-green was on a half-price sale. And on top of that you can still bargain with the Indians about the price. I have never been good with that. Ester however is. She really can barter. But at home she keeps quiet. We get the best price and they know that we'll be back soon. That's the reason why we have been buying from Moola's for years. That's why they do it.

The inside of the blocks can be multi-coloured from the left-over wool and jerseys that have been unravelled, but the outside, the last row and the edges must be plain. A double-bed cover can cost you two packets. This one is a single for Rika, one of my twenty-two grandchildren's little ones.

Ester will help me make my bed later. Almost like the proverb: You make the bed that you lie in yourself. You don't leave it for someone else to do, especially not the maid. That's how I was brought up and I raised my children in the same way.

Next to me on the table – on a light green crocheted cloth with a pretty pineapple motif – stands my loyal old companion.

We've come a long way together, me and my radio. I've now got a transistor-radio with FM. And it gets its power from an electric plug, believe it or not. Also a blessing. It goes on in the morning as I open my eyes, and off again at night just before I read my Bible. It's no wonder the batteries don't last. And they are so expensive.

"This is my window to the world, Ester," I always remind her when she complains that it's been on too long and too loud. "There's nothing wrong with my hearing. It just sometimes sounds a little muffled, and on top of that, I struggle some nights to fall asleep. It's my Church, my politics; I hear things that women are not meant to talk about; and stories of places and stuff that I now know about, but still not really enough about where and what they are. But they are there. Out there somewhere. It's good to know that."

We have already had TV for many years but it is a night time thing. A togetherness thing. And then you watch what everyone else is watching. But with the radio …

This morning's message was about compassion. The parable about the Good Samaritan who could not pass by was read aloud and reflected on.

Once again they played one of those hymns from the New Hymnbook. I really don't understand what was wrong with the old ones. It was good enough for so many years. The words are still the same but the tune sounds unfamiliar. It's hard for an old dog to learn new tricks. But we'll get used to it.

And then the news came.

By now Emily has already come into the house through the back door, as would be expected from the maid. She makes a bed for the little one on the kitchen floor, just like that, using the blankets which she had used to wrap him tightly onto her back.

It's a roomy kitchen. Perfect for cooking. The washing up area is separate on the built-in stoep with the Louvre-windows.

It's Saturday and the day begins lazily for everyone.

That is, everyone except Ester.

During the week she leaves early in the morning to work from eight to five in the accounts department in the State Pension Fund offices in town. And in the evenings it's the eternal driving around delivering buckets full of milk to the family. Most of the family live in the area; it's just the eldest who lives far away.

Ester needs to work to keep the pot and the plot cooking. She never complains. I think she actually enjoys it. Away from the silence.

On a Friday afternoon she fetches me, and on a Sunday afternoon before sunset she drops me at Baby, my youngest daughter. Baby was christened Maria Gertruida.

Ester has finished making Paul's breakfast.

She is making dolls' clothes.

Ester's sewing room and Paul's study lie between my bedroom and theirs. It is really nice and convenient there. I am closest to the bathroom, the phone and the kitchen. Its advantage isn't only the distance, but it also buys me a little time.

I don't complain about my eyes. It's just my old legs. They don't always behave. Especially the knees. It's the weight. And sitting around all day doesn't help either. Plus the walking stick can also only do so much. So these days I mostly sit, because I walk with too much difficulty. A person just can't win. Both ways you lose.

Ester can walk straight out of her bedroom into her sewing room through the interleading door. Her workroom is crammed full of dolls and there are more of them on the couch in the lounge. Porcelain dolls. They are such old-fashioned dolls. In my younger days ours were made of cloth. But we had heard of the ones that were made like chinaware.

She embroiders the most delicate little flowers.

Ester's hands can do no wrong. I don't say that because she is my child. If I think back and compare her to now, she leaves me speechless. At school she handed in my handiwork or she would still have been busy today.

Ester has become a good wife to Paul. A very good wife.

Her baking is foolproof. It never flops. She cooks like a dream! What she creates with a flower or a needle is almost an art form.

Luckily this thing with dolls is only a fad. A craze amongst adults.

But with Ester however there are far too many of them.

One thing I know about is needlework. It was one of those things that you had to do. Bought clothes only recently stilled our busy hands. There are few allowances made for people of my proportions and I had to keep sewing as long as I could. It's only wedding clothes that are still made by hand by Missus Human here in Horison.

The dolls were something to fill the emptiness for Ester.

It takes her hours and hours of patience: with felt, silk thread, cross stitch that runs in perfect rows and in the same direction, smocking, crotchet work, knitting, stitching by hand or machine; from blouses of silky fabric through to three-piece suits made of the finest single-ply wool or cotton on her Empisal; through to wall-hangings suspended on a copper pipe or framed behind glass.

She is always one up on me. Now that it's winter it's because she is younger, and doesn't need glasses or a reading lamp. In the warm months with its early mornings my hands become fidgety from about five-thirty and I find myself at a loss. First things first. First listen to the morning message. Five to six. It's then that the house stops dead. Then, as on a Sunday, you dare not touch a needle, be it for sewing, knitting or crocheting, no matter how your hands are itching to, because that is like stabbing it into the eye of God. I drummed this into my daughters from an early age.

It's the theme-tune that stops you in your tracks and the closing hymn that starts you up again. After that everyone walks on tip-toe through the house, with one ear glued to the radio, because come six o-'clock they tell you what is happening in your world.

By this time I've already gone about my business and start to unravel my wool.

This morning's news is that the country is having an "emergency" because it is in a "state," or so the joke goes about the State of Emergency we are in.

And then we do what we have to do. We make them

a kraal *(coral)*. Just like we do for the cattle. We chase them in. Then we count them carefully. In this way we are sure that they are out of the way for the night and we know exactly where they are and what they could possibly get up to. According to Botha it's in at seven o'clock and out again at five o'clock. The rule even applies to Emily and Amos. They have to be on this side of the fence between these times or they get caught and fined.

Emily is busy with the dishes from supper the night before. The tap runs and she washes.

She gazes out of the window in the direction that Paul is walking through the flat, open *veld*. Like a ghost he disappears underground. It is as if the earth has swallowed him up. The soap-suds pour over the edge of the basin, but she doesn't seem to notice.

She stares.

She stares beyond the horizon.

Paul climbs down a ladder into a man-made hole, two and a half metres deep and six by four metres wide. It's like a huge swimming pool. Inside the hole he "Good morning's" Amos who is raking hay, and throws the contents of his buckets into a trough.

"One of these days, listen carefully, one day the police are still going to catch us, Master Paul," Amos says knowingly. "It's the law."

He is referring to the three pigs that Paul is busy feeding.

"You can keep cows and sheep, but not pigs. It's because they stink and they carry disease."

"My pigs ..." Paul protests in vain.

"You're still not allowed to keep them in the middle of the town, my Master!"

Paul finds it funny that this youngster is trying to lecture him. He, of all people, knows better.

"My pigs don't stink," he says as a father would to a child. "They are clean and healthy. I know what a clean pig looks like. I write about them – for the newspapers, remember, – for almost thirty years I have been writing about pigs."

Paul laughs because he knows it is true. He retired from *The Star* twelve years ago, where he was editor of the agricultural section.

"But it's the law," groans Amos with a strained laugh.

Paul runs his own small knock-and-drop newspaper here in the area, more because he feels that he still can work, and because he can never sit still. Now he writes about any- and everything.

"I also write about the people who make the laws. I don't think there is a single pig in this country that I haven't written about."

He laughs.

"But we live in the city, my Master."

Amos gestures in the general direction of Ontdekkers Road, a dual-carriage main road that runs straight past the plot. When travelling from Krugersdorp, there are exactly thirty-four traffic lights along Ontdekkers Road and suddenly you're in the Johannesburg city-centre without having turned left or right. By seven o'clock in the morning it feels as if everyone in Krugersdorp has flooded the city and everyone inside it needs to flee. In this direction.

"Amos, there are more important things at the moment than a few pigs that the government and police should be busying themselves with."

They have had this conversation before.

"But it's the law, Master Paul!" Amos is now practically singing his plea.

Paul finds it funny.

"If the government can bend the law, then we can all bend it together. How will the police find out? It's only you, Miss Ester and I who know about this. Not even the Old Missus or Emily, not to mention the rest of the family, even suspect a thing. What the eye doesn't see doesn't hurt the heart, Amos," consoles Paul.

It was in fact months later, around slaughtering time, that I found out that there were pigs in the vicinity. At a glance it looked like an insignificant piece of land with tall yellow grass. That's all.

Paul and his bending of the rules was a new development.

Emily stares totally lost in the direction that Paul has disappeared in. The tap keeps running. The soap-suds cascade over the edge. She doesn't even realise that she is standing in a pool of water. It is the soap that caused the plate to slip out of her hands.

All hell breaks loose. Emily starts screaming. The child, scared out of his wits, screams loudly in unison. Between the two of them they practically raise the roof. Emily tears out the backdoor, screaming as she goes. As far as she runs, she rips the clothes off her body as if they are burning coals, all along the track on her way to the gate.

Ester gets up, dead calm, and walks out the room as if nothing has happened. She walks into the kitchen. She sees the shattered plate. She picks up the child and puts him on her hip.

The heads of both Paul and Amos suddenly pop up above the ground, like two rabbits emerging from their burrow.

I struggle to my feet and slowly make my way to the window, open the curtain and look out. I'm not just peeping through the burglar bars, I am really looking. We were taught after all that peeping is a bad thing.

By this time Emily is standing naked as Eve in all her glory in the field.

She suddenly stops, turns slowly and begins staring at the house as if she's seen a ghost.

Paul is blindly looking at her. He's halfway out of the hole. He doesn't seem to be in any hurry.

Amos also seems to get moving almost reluctantly.

Emily stands in the middle of nowhere swaying from side to side as if she is busy dancing. She mumbles the song that she was singing earlier to something or someone inside her head.

I grab my walking stick and shuffle down the passage, bumping into Ester. She is on the telephone. In one hand she has the receiver and in the other arm, the child.

"It's enough now, Ma *(Mom)*. We need help before it's too late. Hello, its Missus De Villiers here, can you please ..." She explains the situation to the people from Emergency Services on the other end of the line and rattles off the address to them. And with that, she is out the door.

"It's the same old story every day and it is just getting worse and worse!" is the last that I hear.

It's early, its Saturday and its quiet, except of course for Emily. By the time I've made my way down the stairs, I can hear the ambulance approaching from far away.

As I round the corner I hear Paul's bruskness.

"Leave the child, Ester. Put him down."

Ester, in the manner of a woman, casts her eyes down. Also in the manner of a woman, she ignores him.

"He's just a child, Paul," she says so as not to frighten the child. Soft and firm.

"But he is, and always will be a *kaffertjie.*"

Her eyes burn right through him.

The wail of the ambulance is almost at the gate.

"Paul, have you forgotten ..." is all that she can manage.

It is clear enough for him.

He sees something in her that he doesn't recognise. Her love for him has always gone hand in hand with respect. Child and parent.

"One day ... one day he will slit your throat."

She can only stare at him mutely. It's almost as if she feels pity for him.

"If it wasn't for you ... we would have had our own," she mouths at him. There is no bitterness. Just cold fact.

He doesn't hear her. The wail of the ambulance silences her mute words.

But I hear.

By this time the ambulance-men have got Emily under control and have restrained her. It doesn't matter to her anymore. They try to help her into the ambulance. Amos also lends a hand.

"I must go to work. We'll talk about it. Later." Paul turns around and walks towards the house.

As Emily puts her foot into the ambulance, she suddenly stops dead. She turns on the spot and screams like a mad woman: "Miss Ester! Miss Ester, look after my child!"

Paul freezes in his tracks.

After the ambulance left with Emily and Amos and everything was back to normal, Paul took off in his green Mazda to find the rest of his story who knows where.

Just last night at the dinner table he was telling Ester and I the thing about the Drakensberger breed of cattle. Paul can talk about bird and beast like no woman can about a winning recipe. It is like he is young again. He leans forward enthusiastically with his elbows on the table and rubs his hands together with pleasure.

"I remember it like it was today. It was in 1973 that I saw the Drakensberger for the first time."

He tells a good story. He always looks at me first and then at Ester to make sure that we are all ears.

"It was at the Rand Easter Show. About a year or so earlier the South African Stud Society recognised them as a breed for the first time."

He folds his serviette and places it on his side plate. A fastidious man.

"It's rather ironic if a person thinks about it that they have been here in the region for longer than we care to admit." He holds my gaze: "Mother, think of the most, most beautiful and blacker than black bull – and believe me he is blacker than that. Mother, think about the bulls of Spain!" He is suddenly a child once more.

And I get a picture in my mind. One from the radio. One from books and one from the TV. But it's the image of the silk tapestry of the Fighter and the Beast against Betta, my eldest's lounge wall – she was christened Elisabetta –

that captures my imagination. I pity the poor eyes that had to stitch with that black thread.

"When the Dutch landed here, the Drakensbergers were already here on the Cape Flats. And even earlier, Da Gama, the Portuguese explorer, wrote a report on them."

He knows and enjoys his story.

"Funnily enough, they are commonly known as the 'Black Afrikaner.'"

He laughs, turns around and puts the TV on in the lounge. He can see that I can see him through the open double doors. He's rather early. The adverts are still on.

"At that stage there were only fourteen Drakensbergers against the seventeen hundred others who officially took part in the show."

He walks past and picks up the tray with the crockery and carries it into the kitchen.

When I was a young girl a man only ever put his foot in the kitchen if he was on his way to the backdoor.

With me around, with only one hand free to keep me standing, Paul doesn't hesitate on a Sunday afternoon to put an apron on over his church pants, shirt and tie, and with a dish towel in hand helps to dry the dishes. It's the Day of Rest and that applies to the hired help as well.

On his return he says: "And now they are everywhere. You can't miss them anymore." He walks off laughing at his own joke and sits down in his chair. The news has started. The focus is on the State of Emergency.

I disappear and join Ester in the kitchen for company. I'm going to hear it again tomorrow morning anyway.

It wasn't yet late enough for me to read my Bible, but

it was later than usual, because I was still listening to a story or two when I heard Paul on the phone right outside my door.

We have never lived with closed doors. When I go to sleep at night I open my door a little. That means: Goodnight, I've gone to sleep so leave me alone but if you have to, you can come in. Or something like that. I do it straight away when I come back from the dining room and after that, the bathroom. Close it just enough. I walk and put the bedside light on and pull the small table with my radio on it closer. With all the lights blazing I do my thing and finally I switch the main light off at the wall. Everything is now comfortably within reach and then I climb into bed.

He can clearly see that my light is still on and that the door is slightly ajar, but it's as if he deliberately talks louder every time that I crank the radio up. So I give up and turn it down before Ester complains again.

Well, I tried not to eavesdrop.

Practically before the phone was answered he started: "The country's burning and there is nothing we can do about it. This government is busy tying our hands behind our backs."

These days all conversations seem to begin with what is closest to our hearts: "Our country is ..." Everyone's hearts are brimming over with it. "Burning" at the beginning and "bankrupt" by the end.

"We can talk about it, behind closed doors, as long as we don't write about it. Today you can't write about this, and tomorrow it is that. One day people are going to say, and no-one will believe them, that they were kept in the dark about it. They didn't know what was happening in this country of ours."

And I hear him talking about things that we as women must be protected from.

He and I could talk – there was a mere ten years or so between us – and when you're as old as I am, you are allowed to voice your deceased husband's opinions in his absence and venture to ask a few questions on behalf of the family. This frankness was allowed.

Ester was brought up a SAP *(South African Party)* and he a Nationalist.

"What does your heart say, Paul?" I had asked him this direct and weighty question before.

He knelt at my side, took both of my hands in his and looked me in the eyes.

"I promised myself that as long as I am a journalist, I won't choose sides, that I will remain neutral."

I was content with that.

The women kept their heads in the sand. In front of the men, that is. We were excluded from religious and political discussions. The men's reasoning was always that it led to a fight and that it was better for us and the children to stay out of it.

It became a kind of routine. A woman walks in and the topic of conversation changes without the men batting an eyelid. Little did the men realise what we speculated about amongst ourselves when they weren't around.

Ester would never dare to voice her opinion in front of Paul.

There were unfortunately those amongst the fairer sex who found it convenient for the men to think on their behalf.

"All we can do now is stand and watch. Watch a

revolution brewing right here under our noses," he roars above the volume of my radio. "But it is getting harder for me to hold my tongue!" And in the same breath he arranges to pick up the person on the other side of the line the next day to take photos of the ever-present Drakensberger.

By this time they are probably there already.

Halfway down the passage I can hear Ester making "coo-ing" noises. A little one in the house seems to turn adults into imbeciles who each talk to an infant in their own kind of baby talk. We seem to think that they understand things like "goo-goo."

Ester is bent over the *kaffertjie* who is lying stark-naked on her and Paul's bed. There she stands struggling with his nappy. I think to myself: If Paul could only see this he would have a heart attack!

I carefully edge closer and tap my walking stick lightly on the door to let her know I am there. I obviously need to help her with this fumbling, but I also don't want it to look like I'm interfering. She obviously doesn't have a clue what to do.

I fold the lowest point of the triangle of the nappy under his bottom so that she can see.

"I heard what you said, Ester."

At the same time I fold the left-hand over the right-hand corner and close the nappy over his tummy.

"You knew."

And I show her how to push the safety-pin through. Then I undo it so that she can try from scratch.

"You always knew that the two of you would never be able to have children ... Start with the bottom corner. First there were the dogs. Eighteen at the very least. Left over right."

You only ever need to show her how to do something once. She has it taped.

"Twenty-one to be precise," she says proudly as she closes the nappy.

"Twenty-one then. And then you started with the dolls. I saw how you changed into … What was his name again?"

"Who's name, Ma?" she says pretending not to understand.

"The man who made Pinocchio."

"Giopetto, Ma," and Ester pushes the safety-pin through.

"Giopetto. Ester, the day Paul asked for your hand in marriage, your late father and I were very surprised. No, we were actually worried."

"Because he'd been married before, Ma?"

"Yes and no. We knew her. You knew her. How could it be any different? She was after all the neighbours across the road's daughter. Everyone had accepted that if he married again, he would marry the teacher who was boarding with Uncle Flip's other daughter. Paul was an educated man. A man with a degree. And at least she was a bit older and had a higher-education. What's more, you were still at school. You weren't even eighteen and he was a man of nearly forty, when he started courting you."

"We waited for nearly three years. And now it's almost thirty years later."

"He was a widower. And they were also childless."

And then the awkwardness starts with the baby's bottle. It is standing in hot water, but what to do next?

"Like this." I squirt a bit of milk onto my hand, and

she copies me.

"At least they adopted one ... Herbert."

And saying this, she plugs the baby's mouth with the bottle.

"Ma, you of all people should know how I feel about Herbert. The fact that he's German and a war-orphan to boot is not the problem."

She paces back and forth on the carpet while rocking the child.

"The fact that we're the same age is not the problem. The fact that he feels threatened by my very presence ... is his problem."

And with every turn she reels off the options.

Now I'm confused.

"So, what is the problem then?"

"Paul at least knows what it feels like to be a father, Mother!" she says spitting out every word. Her nostrils flare. Her eyes flash.

This is how she shuts me up.

I realise that she chose this path knowing full well that there would never be any children. I wouldn't know what it feels like. Never. Not even remotely. I'm on the other end of the scale. I've already buried more than half of my own. Is one heartache worse than the other? Is it possible for one to outweigh the other?

And Ester does what she was born to do. She rocks him to sleep.

And the whole time that we are standing and bandying words about, I could not help wondering over and over: How does it feel to touch a *kaffertjie* in this way? My head was filled with thoughts of how filthy they are; how they stink and all the lice and other diseases that they carry.

We had always been told this. And it is true. But it hadn't always been like that.

In my day with the coal-stove in the house and the petrol drums they used to make fire in their huts, the smell of smoke was in everybody's bedding, clothing and hair. It was fire after all that provided hot water and food for all of us. Coal and wood. And the paraffin for the lamps and candles left everyone smelling slightly stuffy.

Water was carried by hand. We all had to carry our water, as everyone lived the same distance from the water pump.

The soap that we brewed in a three-legged pot out of pig fat and bicarbonate-of-soda under a tree – even here in the city under the old Apricot tree in the back corner of the yard – was liberally handed out to everyone.

Lice were brought home from school. It was always the offspring of the poorest of the poor that carried it.

The drought scared all my adolescent children away from Swartruggens and they fled to the city to find work. A season later, with the last of the scorched corn still in the fields, we also landed in Unified, a stone's throw away from the children. Along with Uncle Flip's family diagonally across the road. And Paul.

Here we had electricity for the first time. You turned the stove on at the wall and somewhere in the ceiling a big kettle boiled water for the bath and the dishes which poured out from a mere twist of the tap. Hot and cold. The days of making bars of soap that smelt of cleanliness were numbered, and you could pick and choose bars of every colour and scent from any Greek corner café and even had a choice between Jayes and Dettol for disinfecting.

Suddenly we discovered that we had a different smell. Better. Now we smell sweet.

And if you take into account how we battled to get our husbands and sons to use the underarm stuff. How easily we forget!

But these things don't seem to bother Ester.

One thing I know: Ester would have made a good mother.

Ester cleans up the mess on the floor and takes over where Emily left off with the dishes. I make myself useful and pour us a cup of tea. I'm here every weekend and still every time she treats me like I'm a guest. She takes out the best china.

The tray has a tray-cloth the milk jug has a doily; the teapot is first rinsed out with boiling water, and the matching Royal Albert teaspoons with the matching porcelain face which matches the cups and saucers all lie in the same direction. The milk is already poured ready for your first cup.

You'll never find anything like a shop-bought biscuit in her home. With tea you always get a slice of cake, a tart or something savoury, and a Rusk with your coffee. She makes her coffee with hot milk.

On the floor to the side the child lies on his bundle of blankets, fast asleep. There's a sense of warmth in the kitchen.

Out of the blue she starts.

"I will never understand the blacks. They are different to us."

"We're all the same in God's eyes," I remind her.

"That's not what I mean."

I am glad to hear that. That's not how we raised her.

I make myself comfortable on a high stool that they keep in the kitchen especially for me.

"The child was barely seven months old – I remember it vividly – when they upped and left, and then they were gone."

Ester dries the dishes one by one and packs them away in the same manner.

"Who?" I want to know.

"Patricia and the child, Ma," she replies on her way to the cupboard.

"Patricia who?"

"Amos' mother," she says on her way back to the sink. "Do you still remember what she did?" This time she stops for just a moment. "She came to help with the child's birth and to look after it. And when she left, she packed the child up with her without saying a word."

"That's what they do, my child."

I don't think that's what she wants to hear.

Now it's time for the side-plates. One by one.

"I know that. I know the story – that the Ouma (Grandmother) brings up the child – but why, why in the Transkei of all places – it's almost twelve hundred kilometres from here – and why Patricia? It's beyond my understanding."

When it comes to this, we are like peas in a pod, I think to myself.

"Do you have any idea how many times I've had to look after my grandchildren, h'm?"

That's the only benefit of being an Ouma. This is how I get the chance to spend so much time with them.

"I'm not complaining."

"It's different. You were always a stone's throw away."

"Convenient, hey," I plant the seed.

"What I don't understand is this: How can a mother let tradition part her from her own flesh and blood? You would think Amos would have known better by then."

Finally she stops pacing to and fro. She folds her dishcloth.

"Emily ... ah ... Emily. You can't hold it against her either. She'd already lost her marbles," sighs Ester.

The child starts crying. Ester picks him up, tests the milk on her hand and gives him his bottle.

Here we go again. Back and forth. Up and down. Up and down while she pacifies the child. And as the child calms down, so does she.

In passing she switches on the light.

Along with the late sunrise comes the early dusk. The dying of the day always rewards us with a golden glow. That's when the world transforms into pure Africa. The sun doesn't sink, it falls. It's fleeting. And then it's gone.

"I remember it as if it were yesterday. Amos was busy digging in the garden, Ma. If there's something that I can't stand, it's a man who doesn't know what to do with a spade."

I have to laugh.

"The man who can handle a spade as well as you can has yet to be born."

Ester has to laugh.

"And I'm too old and tired to teach a man what to do. I grabbed the spade from him and started digging. I told him to walk behind me and pick up the weeds in my wake."

"It must have been hell for him to keep up," I add and double over with laughter.

They shared a passion. Gardening. What Ester didn't know about gardening, she was quick to learn. She's not shy to ask if she wants to know something.

Their closest neighbour was a nursery. Lantana.

All that was here when they moved in were the ancient Blue Gum trees at the gate, the fruit trees and the massive Loquat tree outside the backdoor which provided shade.

They planted trees and shrubs absolutely everywhere. Petunias, Impatiens and Pansies were handed over the fence to Ester to give the garden colour. Borehole water was used to soak the ground. Sparingly but often. Wheelbarrow loads of cow dung were dug into the ground. And with Ester as the chief digger, the cows could barely keep up. A feast for the eye. So beautiful. Even in the winter months with Coxcombs in blood-red, orange and yellow, one could easily look straight past the lifeless lawn.

Ester can aim with her eye, push with her foot and send a spade straight into the ground without so much as a by your leave. She digs without looking back. It's as if the Devil of Digging possesses her and needs to get out.

"If you slice it into the ground in one movement until your foot is level with the ground," she explains, "then you can be certain that you have outsmarted the rock, the gravel, roots or whatever else might be in your path."

Ester starts laughing. She can't help herself.

"It was then that he told me that the child had fallen into the fire and had burnt his backside. I almost exploded. My first reaction was to ask him what the sense was of leaving a child with an Ouma who was incapable of looking after him properly. It was when he told me that the wound had gone septic and wasn't getting better that I did explode. They hadn't taken him to a doctor. They tried to heal him in the 'traditional' way."

Her laughter reaches a climax.

And stops as suddenly.

"And it didn't work, Ma. I called Paul and we forced them to go and fetch the child."

There is a knock at the door.

Ester goes to the door.

She calls softly: "Amos, is it you?"

And from outside the door you hear: "Yes, Miss Ester."

Ester opens the door.

Amos comes inside.

"I've come for the child. Good evening, Old Missus," he greets, with his hat in his hand.

I greet him back. And I ask about Emily.

"She's well, Old Missus. She'll sleep well tonight."

Ester hands him the child.

He leaves.

My eyes might be failing, my legs too, but there's nothing wrong with my sense of smell.

"He reeks of alcohol. When did that start?" I ask Ester in case she hasn't picked anything up.

"I don't know."

Now she's tidying up all the tea things.

"And what does Paul have to say about it?"

"What can he say, Ma?"

Paul's the one who always said that he'd employed him because he doesn't drink or smoke.

"Paul doesn't like it, but on the other hand it's not

affecting his work, and you know, Ma, how Paul feels about his little angel. I wonder what's keeping him so long? It's already time for the news. Let me help you up, Ma."

Amos was a man of and for the earth. Paul hails from Wolmaransstad in the Transvaal *(Gauteng)* and Amos from somewhere in the Transkei *(Eastern Cape)*.

Paul's parents counted as part of the 300 000 poor-whites who by 1932 were already living below the breadline.

For us it was also an uphill battle.

His people were paralysed by poverty. Squatters on our own land.

In the year that the depression was at its worst, God's Word appeared in our mother tongue for the first time.

Then the big exodus began. To the city.

Amongst us Afrikaners we called Johannesburg "Judasburg." The city of the English and the Jews. Here we got to see the enemy eye to eye. The political landscape was changing. Our people got their spirit back. Things were going much, much, better, thank you very much. And we were no longer ashamed to speak our own language on the streets.

When Amos came looking for work, Paul was touched by his misery. He had also not been able to sever the umbilical cord from Mother Earth. The drought in the Transkei had dragged him here.

The city was a wake-up call for everyone.

We were here to stay. And so we had to find a way to fit in.

Amos however was defeated by the City of Gold and had come to Paul looking for something to remind him of home.

Paul recognised this in him.

The city had the exact opposite effect on the blacks as on the whites. The blacks quickly learnt all the bad habits of the whites. They started drinking, gambling and committing adultery.

In contrast to this, the Afrikaner however strengthened his grip on the Bible.

The news starts. Both sets of hands get busy with our hobbies. Ester is making another doll's dress and I'm still busy with the blanket. I'm attaching the blocks to one another. At least it's now big enough to keep my legs warm. Snug in the winter but stifling in the summer.

On the screen the Comrades are crawling all over the place, stoning the police cars and the armoured vehicles. Soldiers with guns appear on the scene. Everywhere you look are children running away. It's been going on like this in Alexandra for what seems like forever. They've got something against the State of Emergency and are attempting to destabilise the country. Everything is out of control. Wherever you look the country is burning. Oppressive black smoke billows from all the burning tyres.

Ester gets up and goes to the front door.

"Ma, it's children. It's children who are fighting like this. I can't look. The war is being waged by children. Children who feel their parents aren't doing enough. Children are being thrown into prison without trial, Ma."

She turns the door handle. It's locked. There are three different locks on the door. She checks them all. One by one. She walks back to the lounge, stops in her tracks, and stares out the window.

"The youngest detainee is only eight years old," says Paul.

She stares out the window for an eternity. Staring in the direction of the servants' quarters. A light is burning.

It is the crying of the child that catches her attention.

It is also one of those windows with lots of security bars. In the light from outside they look like prison bars.

"I wonder what Emily and Amos must think when they see things like this," she says.

She draws the curtains.

"You'll never know. We taught the blacks well. We trained them to say: 'Yes, Master; No, Master' without knowing what they really mean."

"Emily and Amos are different," she says impatiently.

"Different to what?"

"The masses in the locations, Ma."

Also true.

These here and around us, we know. Here in the city every house has a room in the backyard. They are your closest neighbours.

My Bettie, from the days of my husband and I, was inherited first by my one daughter and then by my grandchild. She feels like family. They were always so close that you could call for them from your bedroom window.

And then they say that we live separately.

She was in the house most of the time. She could tell me exactly what was in what drawer. This was as a result of her duties and not because she was nosey. Even what was in the drawer right next to my bed. That close.

Together.

"But they are and always will be black," I explain as I see it. "And at the moment blacks are in revolt and not without reason! For years now we white people have been telling them where they can go and what they can do. They are tired of being treated like children. If you treat adults like children, they will behave like children. This is what these laws boil down to."

Paul is late. It's the beams of the Mazda's lights flickering against the curtains that wake me out of my restless sleep. A person remains restless until all the children are home. It's in our nature.

And this one is already seventy.

He yells "Ester, Mother," from the back door all the way to where I am. Louder and louder. He barges into my room. My heart skips a beat from fright. This block of a man appears like an apparition in the doorway with the light from the passage behind him illuminating him.

"Mother?" he calls into the darkness.

"Evening, Paul," I call back as loudly as I can with a lump in my throat so that he knows I'm there.

"Where's Ester, Mother?"

Fear engulfs me.

Earlier I could see the light shining further down the passage. I heard her working until I dosed off.

"The backdoor's wide open, Mother."

He goes down the passage with "Ester, Ester, Ester" echoing in my ears, getting softer as he goes. When the "Ester's" get louder and louder again I know that something is wrong.

By now I'm sitting up on the side of my bed. I want to grab my gown but my legs have turned to jelly. My other hand seems to still be obeying instructions and I place it on the Bible and ask that whatever the trouble is, we be spared it.

His "Ester" rings in the kitchen and at the backdoor the sound of his "Ester" changes.

We were never afraid when it came to locking doors.

In all my years we lived with unlocked car and house doors. Even in the city until very recently. The lock on the chain at the gate was latched but never locked. A key was something used to start an engine. When the children were small it was there to keep them out of the pantry, otherwise the boys ate us out of house and home.

But now things have changed.

"Ester!"

I have never heard him shout so loudly.

"Ester, what do you think you're doing? What is wrong with you? The blacks are still out on the street. They wipe their feet on the State of Emergency. Which part of 'State' and 'Emergency' don't you understand? What are you doing outdoors?"

I stuff the corner of my gown into my mouth and start giggling like a girl from pure relief. And if he adds "and the country is burning" I'll end up swallowing the whole pink affair, flowers and all. That he likes to stand and preach is a way of life for him. If someone doesn't understand, he'll make sure that they do. A serious thing like this could go on for as long as a Communion Service.

Ester was playing with her dolls earlier while sitting and waiting for Paul. She wasn't concerned that he was late. It's part of what he does. His time away is her alone time.

But not tonight.

When a sound disturbs you out of the silence, and you start listening, it gets louder and louder, drowning out everything else. That's exactly the effect that the little one's wail has on her. Firstly a far off sound in the distance and then drumming inside her head. The crying awakens her senses to Emily's earlier plea: "Miss Ester, Miss Ester, take care of my child."

She loses her will and follows the sound.

She rushes out the back door into the cold without her jersey. Crossing the yard in her socks, she stops outside the Xele's room. Here she stands dead still and listens. She's afraid that her imagination has got the better of her.

Once she is certain, she knocks tentatively on the door.

Nothing stirs. And the screaming continues.

She carefully pushes open the door.

Amos is lying flat on his back with the child in his arms. He is passed out for the night. The child is screaming right into his ear and he hears nothing. He and the drink are sorry partners elsewhere.

She gently picks up the screaming child. Her attention is all that he needed.

She doesn't even hear the Mazda arriving.

At the back door she walks straight into a thunder-cloud.

"What's wrong with you, Ester!" Paul erupts, looking for reason, as she passes him with the child in her arms.

"Look," and she stops in her tracks right outside my door. She can feel his eyes boring through her back. "The only thing wrong with me is that I could no longer bear to hear the wailing of the child." She says this loudly enough for me to hear as well.

She turns, looking straight into his eyes.

Ester's strength lies in her short sentences.

"Have you forgotten about Veronica?" she asks.

And with the child in her arms she heads in the direction of the bedroom. At the door she turns again and faces him head-on.

"I told you before, and I swore before God, that this thing will never again happen near me or in my house." It is her sense of self that gives her the strength to say it.

"You couldn't do anything about it, Ester."

Paul realises that he's standing at the edge of a bottomless pit.

"There was a lot that I could have done if I hadn't blocked my ears to the screaming of the child. I should have known there was a problem. The child never stopped. But I kept telling myself that she was just the servant; she was black, so what did it matter?"

At that time Ester and Paul lived just two blocks away from me. Veronica came on a Saturday to do the washing and the floors. She didn't live in.

This thing still had her in its grip.

"You asked her what was wrong and whether she had taken the child to a doctor. And?"

"She lied!"

Ester kept asking whether Veronica had taken the child to a doctor, and the answer always was: "Yes." Out of desperation this time she bundled Veronica and the child into the car and took them to the doctor. It materialised from the examination that the child was suffering from malnutrition.

Instead of buying food, Veronica had been drinking her money away.

"It's not your fault," Paul said. He knows the story. He knows her pain.

Ester just looks at him. She shakes her head out of despondency.

"It's not your fault that she squandered all her money on drink."

"I smelt it and I did nothing."

"I have been writing for the last how many years that our people spend more money on drink than on red meat." The journalist in Paul begins to spell out the situation for Ester. "Nine Million more Rand this year than last year. Alcohol is at the top of the groceries list. And fifty percent more on tobacco than on vegetables. Every day there are millions of children here, and throughout the world, that are starving and there's nothing that we can do."

"Yes, Paul, people can read and write about the millions, but you have to experience it only once! That child died three days later. It's not going to happen to this one. Not in this house."

She carries the child into the room and dumps him in the middle of the bed.

"Never again!"

Paul's final words for the evening would ring in these passages for a long time to come.

"Who would ever have thought that a *kaffertjie* would one day land in my bed between me and my wife?"

Just after seven I see Ester, with the little one, walking in the direction of the cattle *kraal*.

Amos is busy milking when he sees her coming.

Head bowed with hat in hand, he awkwardly stands closer.

"Miss Ester, I am so sorry ..."

Ester does not set great store by apologies. Paul neither. As a situation rears its ugly head, it is dealt with. It doesn't get dwelt upon. "Work at the solution and the problem is soon forgotten," Paul always says in his wisdom.

"It doesn't matter, Amos. I spoke to Master Paul and he agreed that we must do what needs to be done."

Ester makes a bed for the child on the grass.

"Amos, we will help you where and when we can. At least until Emily is better."

"That will never ..."

Ester interrupts him. She isn't in the mood for a story.

I will ask Master Sarel to help you during the day, while I'm at work. At night or on weekends, or whenever, he is welcome to stay with us in the house. Master Paul agrees."

Ester cups her hand over her mouth. She tries hard to suppress the laughter gurgling in her throat. In this manner she scurries back to the house like someone who is choking. At the corner of the house she lets it all out. Gee, this child of mine has an infectious laugh.

It's Sunday and everything is organised, firstly for Church, and thereafter for the family invasion.

When my husband was still alive, and we still had our own home, the gathering of the clan was at our place every second Sunday. Our children and their families almost numbered close to fifty then.

"It's also right that they come here now," Paul replied when I once asked them about the inconvenience that I was causing them.

I have stopped counting. I'm sure they now number close to eighty. I already have sixteen great-great-grand-children.

"The house is big, and there's more than enough place for the children to run around in and make a noise. They never all descend on us together anyway. They come to visit you, Mother. And you get a chance to see them all."

We're eating early today, while there's still sun.

Usually everybody chips in for Sunday lunch. My daughters and daughters-in-law all arrive with dishes brimming with the tastiest of tasty food. Everyone makes a lot of one dish and in this way the women's hands also get a chance to rest a bit on the Sabbath. It's almost impossible to get a spoonful of everything onto your plate, because of the large variety. There are green beans with potatoes and bacon; potato salad with homemade and bought mayonnaise; bean salad cooked through the night, not out of a tin; avocado in aspic; beetroot salad with onions; grated carrots with pineapple; curried peaches with samp; you name it and we have it.

And after lunch, all the leftovers are divided into equal portions for supper. You never go home with an empty bowl.

Puddings, baked and set, are in abundance to choose from. There is never any sibling rivalry and recipes are happily exchanged. It is clear who makes what the best.

The men stand and braai (barbeque). Outside the kitchen in front of an open fire the men are kings of their castle. The mouth-watering smell of sausage; lamb chops and steak invade the senses. The tables are already laid under the Loquat Tree. It's a feast for nearly thirty.

Ester is busy in the kitchen.

Baby and Betta's lot are all here for a change, and Marieke, Sarel, my second youngest's Dutch-born wife, is also giving a helping hand.

It's then that Baby volunteers the story. They would never relate something like this in front of me.

"Do you know, the other day I heard the funniest story from a friend of mine. It happened to her friend's friends. You know how we let the maids do just what they want to in our homes. They take coffee and bread and ..."

"Sugar never lasts in my house," adds Marieke. She is a Hollander and something like this would worry her. She stirs the white sauce for the cauliflower more intensely.

"Not to mention the telephone. They spend hours and hours on the phone talking at the tops of their voices," Betta moans over her shoulder while packing the plates into the warm drawer.

Warm plates are important especially in the winter. Then the food doesn't get cold. The side plates for the salad are another story.

"Exactly," Marieke calls out. "It's only because they don't have to pay for it," she says while pouring a little more milk into the sauce, because it's starting to look more like porridge. This happens if you over-do the flour in the beginning. "And the same goes for the electricity. They never put a light off. And water! They of course think we get it for free!" she says looking pleased with her handiwork.

It's unfortunately true. As soon as a person brings home the coffee and stuff, a portion of it is immediately on its way somewhere else, where it is apparently needed more.

I just let my Bettie say her say. I held my tongue as

long as they took turns calling. Then it only cost half. Her family was spread far and wide. A person had to accept it like that.

The water and lights? Talking only helped for a short while.

But these are difficult times.

"Every week things get more and more expensive. Just look at what we pay for a loaf of bread these days, not to mention sugar and milk," Marieke complains.

"Double," Betta sighs.

"It's all petrol's fault," everybody complains together.

"Ever since nobody wants to sell us oil anymore, everything's just gone up and up! And when the petrol price goes up, everything is more expensive within the week," Paul had complained to me a week or so before.

I was busy unravelling an old jersey, and as with my deceased husband, Paul's hands were on standby so that I could wind the wool around them. First a person makes a long spool; then you wash the wool to get all the kinks out; and finally you roll it into balls.

"The country is bankrupt. This thing is costing us a fortune. In the beginning it was guns and ammunition; then sport, and then Iraq and Iran started on about the oil. Now it's culture's turn. And the Church's." He sighs. "Now we must just wait and see what's next. We pay through our teeth for everything that we want." He takes one of the spools and first winds it around his hand to start a new ball. "But these boycotts are also just as thin as the paper that our money is printed on, Mother. Look at the Hollanders and how they're moaning about what's going on here. They were the last to jump in and now they're boycotting us with culture. It doesn't concern us. We didn't retain anything of theirs. The English made sure of that." Paul is weighed down about things like this and he winds the wool even tighter. "There is a Makro and a Shell on every corner!" And Paul starts sounding like he is holding a political rally just for my sake. "The same goes for computers. The United Nations are shouting their mouths off about boycotts but no-one is listening. America and England provide and provide, because they know that we're the third biggest buyer in the world. It is common knowledge that the army and the police use computers to control *Apartheid.* Then the exporters got caught out." He gets so carried away with his story that he forgets about the wool. "Their sales to other countries are under threat and they get forced to join in." And he begins winding up again. "What we can no longer buy directly from these countries comes to us via Israel and Taiwan. But will they accept responsibility for their part in the so-called suppression? No!" he says disparagingly and puts the finished ball on one side. "It's all about money, money and more money. The hypocrites!"

He starts laughing quietly. I at first think the man is in tears again.

"But a *'boer'* makes a plan, Mother. Previously they said we were fence-sitters, playing games with each other's heads." And he makes a joke that I don't quite understand. "With sport and everything else we end up playing with our own heads. There's a new name for our national sport ..." and he laughs until he cries.

He continues his train of thought while wiping his eyes with the back of his hand.

"From 1948 they kept us apart through the law."

Paul is an old hand at winding up and knows that the ball is big enough when he comes to the second join. Two ounces. No-one talks about kilograms when it comes to wool. Now again around the hand.

"It was also like that before. Under English rule. 'Separate Development.' Birds of a feather … And then we arrived. And we gave it a name. And *'Apartheid'* became a curse."

Baby was the last to leave home. The last of my children finished school here in the city just like Ester did. Suddenly the house was empty. We were never well-off, but also never went without. Keeping up was hard. And to ease the burden, came the tenants.

At one time we had Mister and Missus Wilson, an English couple. They were a little younger than we were and the perfect companions.

The problem was that my Joshua and I could understand the English, but could never get beyond "Yes" and "No" when it came to answering. They had exactly the same problem with Afrikaans, and suddenly we had a solution. We didn't let this little difference keep us apart. Each spoke their own language. Only slower.

It was Missus Wilson who put it in perspective for me one day, over a cup of coffee.

She said the problem was with the word. It can fall on the English ear in a variety of ways. Where they came from that word started getting its own meaning. They had heard Afrikaans here for the first time. They left Rhodesia *(Zimbabwe)* with just the clothes on their backs when things started hotting up there. Their stories left me feeling sick to my stomach on many an occasion. As with Angola, and more recently with our neighbours in South West Africa *(Namibia)*, everyone was moving south.

With things looking like they are here at the moment, we'll very soon be standing with our backs to the sea. It's this fact that makes people dig their heels in and start grumbling.

She takes *Apartheid* and gives it two meanings. The problem starts with the *"heid."*

"It sounds like we hate them," she says swallowing hard. She uses "we," as they already feel like citizens. "'Apart' too is a problem within itself. It sounds like we are separated by hate. Not guilty!"

It's when she breaks the word up into three parts that I begin to get the picture.

"Look," she says as she writes it down for me. "A-part-hate." That's how she hears it in English.

"Sounds better. Where there is a part hate, there is always a part love too ..."

In her mind, there was a light at the end of the tunnel.

Paul has really found his stride.

"That one word has made us the piss-hole of the world. Excuse my French, Mother, but that's how it makes me feel."

It's one of those words.

Swearing was not in our vocabulary. Not even to yourself.

In my youth, and even later people always "pissed." It wasn't a secret. And it wasn't a rude word either. But somewhere along the way the word had begun to offend people. Suddenly everyone was "wee-ing." It's the same thing. It just sounds better. Then that word also started offending again. I've never known which one is number one and which one number two. It's bad enough that you have to go, but now they want you to specify exactly what you're doing.

I find it offensive!

It's the grandchildren who look at me strangely when the word "piss" slips out occasionally.

"Instead of keeping their own house in order, they point fingers at us," says Paul as he brings me back to the present. "Mother, people don't mix that easily. People all over the world live apart. Overseas they only see the law which makes us worse than them. They call what we are doing here 'inhuman.' And now this same lot are strangling us to death. It's once again the case of the log and the splinter in your own eye. And the joke is that the blacks are suffering – because of the boycotts – as much as we are, if not more. It just makes the natives restless and we're stuck in the middle of everything."

Paul's story and the wool come to an end and he walks out the door.

Baby's not going to let anything stop her in her tracks and plows on with her friend-of-a friend story.

"They do just what they want. My maid, in any case," she says as she chops the parsley finely. "But in our house there is one thing that's taboo – they're not allowed to touch our alcohol. It's the only rule," she says gesturing with the knife.

Everyone agrees.

Paul's reasoning was always that if you don't keep it, then there's no temptation. That was even before the thing with Veronica. All that we ever had in this house was a bottle of sweet wine to accompany Sunday lunch, or Champagne for a special occasion.

"I don't think there's a single house where this rule doesn't apply," says Marieke on behalf of everyone as she pours the sauce over the cauliflower.

"In any case," continues Baby, "they recently invited a few people over for supper. When they finished eating, there was half a bottle of white wine left over. My friend's husband put the cork in and put the bottle back into the fridge. A day or two later he noticed that the bottle was emptier. He asked his wife if she had drunk it – and she denied it – which naturally confirmed his suspicion." And she sprinkles the parsley over the potato salad and garnishes the carrot salad with a whole head of it to make it look pretty.

"So it had to be the maid who worked fulltime for them. She'd been with them for years. I mean, she cooked, cleaned and looked after the children, and because it was the first time that this had happened, the husband decided not to make a fuss about it. But a few days later, he noticed that the bottle was almost empty." By this time Baby has grabbed the bottle of Sunday-wine as she explains further, as if giving a demonstration. "Instead of talking to her about it, he decided to teach her a lesson instead. He took the bottle, opened his fly and filled the bottle. With his own pee!" she ends dramatically.

Everybody finds it hilarious.

"Never," chortles Marieke.

Betta can't believe it and Ester is disgusted.

Marieke nearly pours the whole bottle of nutmeg over the cabbage. Nutmeg gives such a lovely kick and aroma.

"Anyway, he re-corked the bottle and put it back into the fridge. But ... over the next few days the bottle got emptier and emptier. After a few days the bottle was nearly empty again. These friends of mine were gobsmacked!"

Ester might find it funny, but isn't taking the bait.

"Oh, come on, she must've realised that it wasn't wine."

"Well, the man then decided to confront the maid: 'Are you drinking the wine in the fridge?' he asked her."

"'Master knows that I don't drink!' she replied."

"That's what they always say," is Betta's five cents worth, with her hands on her hips.

"By now he was the hell in. He flung the fridge door open and showed her the bottle. 'And how do you explain this then!?' She looked at him in astonishment. 'I don't drink the wine,' she says. 'I cook with it. I put it in your food just like the madam taught me.'"

Betta and Marieke shudder from head to toe.

Ester practically shoves the dishcloth into her mouth to stop herself from laughing.

"It makes you think, doesn't it?" she says as she rushes out the door.

I'm not completely helpless, but with so many pairs of feet in the kitchen, I'm honestly in the way. So I sit outside, with my old body in the sun and my head in the shade of the Loquat tree.

It's only after the laughter here around the corner, for the second time today, that I get to hear the story.

Just then my daughters and Marieke come out of the kitchen. Each with a dish.

"Ma, Ma, I must tell you. It's those three who poured

the wine into the food!" Ester starts again.

Her laughter propels her into the house.

That's one thing about our people. We know how to laugh. Whether at a story or at a joke. At who or whatever's expense.

It is already late when we get to see Amos for the second time during the course of the day. At midday he appears with the child in his arms, to come and fetch a plate of food. The child is completely calm. Marieke ambles over with Ester to look at the child.

At the lunch table I hear Ester hint.

"So if you have any baby clothes that you no longer need, they'll be more than welcome. You saw him – and as you know – he's very tiny for a child of fourteen months."

"I'll see what I can do," Marieke answers.

Marieke's grandchildren, my great-great-grand-children, have been out of their nappies for a long time.

I can see that Ester is ashamed to ask for a change: "I don't want to sound completely dumb but I must admit that I don't have the vaguest idea what a little thing like this needs. What I do know is that Emily has stopped breastfeeding him."

Her eyes cloud over as she contemplates the possibility. "Thank God he's already on the bottle. Everyone always talks about formula and stuff like that. I always thought it was senseless. Until now."

Nobody sees it coming.

When Amos knocks at the back door and Ester opens it for him, I find the answer to the confusion in my head.

With a "Good Evening, Miss Ester," and an "Evening, Amos," he hands over the child and leaves.

Ester blossoms.

The child moves in permanently that evening.

During the following year things change a lot at Ester's.

The child is passed back and forth between willing hands. The little one learns quickly not to discriminate. Hands that give and caress are merely hands.

In the mornings it is Ester who takes him to Amos and later when he gets busy, Sarel helps out. Sarel had found a plot lower down Ontdekkers Road where he keeps livestock, although he doesn't live there. Sarel had taken an early pension due to ill health. He and Amos ride behind the municipal lawnmowers and collect grass for the livestock.

The child gets used to both the shakedown next to Ester's side of the bed and the front seat of a car.

Because Ester delivers milk door-to-door twice week-ly to family and a few friends, the child also gets used to being attached to Ester's hip.

At night after work, the day's milk is divided between a dozen or so white enamel buckets, so that something from the farm can end up in the fridge. For some of the grandchildren who thought that milk came out of a bottle and not out of the udders of a cow, the milk is almost too rich for them. The layer of cream on the milk from the café got thinner and thinner as the milk was watered down. If you didn't know better, you would think that this was so. Ester's cream is so thick that you can almost spread it just like that onto your bread instead of butter.

When Ester does her milk-round almost a month later with the little one, it is Marieke who dares to ask shamelessly: "Why do you do it?"

For a moment it takes the wind out of Ester's sails. "We see it plainly as our Christian duty, Marieke," she says dumbfounded. "It's obvious. We must pitch in until Emily is better."

Then there is the child seat in the shopping trolley where the child sits so comfortably. It is Paul who chooses the toys, and Ester all kinds of treats. The child is mad about Tinkies *(Twinkies)*. He finds that sponge cake with the cream inside delicious. It comes in a handy plastic wrapping and has a long shelf life, or else he would have to wait for the weekend baking.

I'm not sure whether onlookers at that stage found it unusual. Here's a family that at first glance doesn't make any sense. The older man, his daughter and the black child. Wherever they go, the child goes along with them.

And all that he hears is Afrikaans. Maybe that was why he remained silent for such a long time.

Emily wasn't replaced. Everybody's household chores were stretched a bit. There was the expectation that she would get better.

Paul was more often than not in an apron and had mastered the vacuum cleaner.

"Ma, I'll never get anyone again who can iron like Emily," Ester laughs as she stands sweating over the ironing board.

Argh, the ironing. It isn't that it is difficult. The days of warming the iron on the coal stove are gone. You plug it into the wall and it heats itself. You sprinkle water and even the most crinkled cotton lies flat. It still takes patience however. And on top of it all it is soul-destroying, especially when it comes to handkerchiefs and piles of serviettes. The paper version was never an option, not even at a *braai*.

"A monument should be erected for people with her skills," Ester quips when she has finished with the pile.

When Crimplene came in in the seventies and Trilobal in the eighties, my Bettie started smiling again on a Monday.

With my big body and willing hands, plastic material brought other relief. It doesn't fray. You sew straight and it's over. No need to embroider around with zigzag. You stitch the hem too. Suddenly clothes lasted forever and it was more out of boredom than anything else that people went looking for fabric at Moola's. A new design or possibly a different colour. You washed it and hung it up.

My Bettie once shared with me – and for a moment I saw red – that she'd had enough by the time she got to her own housework. That's at her house in the location. Her room here was always spotless.

There wasn't a man in her life. The years of living apart, by law, left her with two daughters that her mother was raising, somewhere in Dobsonville.

All the years under the National Party they had to have permits. To live together. Her husband worked elsewhere and had to live elsewhere too. And this elsewhere led to greener pastures.

The chance for her to visit over weekends was scant with all my children coming over on Sundays. And if Gwyneth or Margaret came to visit with Nora, the Ouma, it was visiting in-between working, and also only for the day. The closest we would come to her house was the police station. If there was a crisis we would drive them there. Transport to that side was difficult and time consuming. But only as far as the police station and no further. Because you see, just as much as they couldn't come and go as they pleased, the same went for us.

If there were only two people in the car, she had to sit in the back, according to the law. A man alone with a black woman was doubly frowned on and judged. In a bakkie they had to sit on the back, like the children.

The road to Dobsonville, from the Roodepoort area, was a familiar road to us. A road familiar through heartache. It was the road to the Roodepoort-West Cemetery. This is where all those who've gone before us, rest.

"They're getting closer and closer. Little by little. You almost don't realise," Baby says referring to the jam-packed houses in the distance.

We usually visit at birthday time. We go bearing flowers to say that we remember.

Gerhard, Marina, my third daughter's husband, went first. Then both my Joshua's. My eldest son with his father's names was the first of my own. Thereafter my other daughter, Milla, and her Christiaan.

It was at Christiaan's burial that Marina walked over to Gerhard's grave knowing that she would be next. Cancer had taken her jawbone and she was so disfigured.

"This is my resting place right here," were her exact words.

Baby quietened her with: "Don't talk like that."

Marina let her prattle on because she knew it was the truth.

There's still rather a distance for me to go.

"What is getting closer?" I want to know.

"Soweto, Ma."

And I look in the direction Baby is looking in.

Once I have seen enough, I look down.

"It was your father's decision to make this his resting place," I say as I examine the headstone next to my deceased husband. "I didn't have much say in the matter." My name is already there. Just the date is missing. It's a strange feeling to stand there and look at something that is still to come. This is where I'm on my way to. You know that with certainty.

"There are so many of them and so few of us," I hear Ester's voice as she painstakingly tends to the flowers, as only she can.

"Ten to one," Marieke quotes the statistics as she hands her the flowers one by one.

The fact that they could have massacred the lot of us by virtue of their numbers, and that it hasn't happened yet remains a miracle in living memory. Like Moses, we are keeping the floods at bay.

You stand and wonder: What exactly am I doing here? Here in this specific place. Here in this country. How did we get here? How do we fit in? Are we guests or are we here to stay? People who live here behave differently to people who are visiting. If we are indeed guests, then we've taken over the whole house.

Alone amongst the dead we women suddenly feel very isolated. And Ester hurries up.

Ester's playing with dolls comes to an end and the dolls disappear into the cupboard one by one. Her sewing is more driven. The clothes are bigger and the right size for her living doll, Raymond.

Raymond is the child's Christian name. His white

name. Vuyo, his black name, is never spoken.

Ester's workroom slowly but surely becomes the child's room and comes to life and gets a small bed. With only a door between them, he is easily within hearing distance.

I find her sitting on the edge of her bed, watching the child sleeping, through the open door.

I imagine she does it often. It's the kind of thing parents do. To make sure the child is still breathing.

"He's like his mother. Beautiful," she says in amazement.

Ester sees it in both of them.

"She was so beautiful when Amos brought her here."

There is something in her that recognises that beauty for what it is and not because she's been told what to say. Somewhere along the road we started believing in our own beauty and that the gene pool that make others different and not fit into our way of seeing things, must obviously be ugly.

The dark skins are one thing. The frizzy hair – another story.

The skin-issue is actually a bit of a joke. The blacks use creams to get whiter, and the whites want to darken themselves at any cost. To be snow-white means that you haven't had a holiday in a long time. It seems that people go on holiday, so that when they come back, they can show others the white patch where their bathing costume kept their modesty out of the sun, in contrast to the pains they went to to burn themselves to a frazzle.

The African sun is merciless to the white skin.

It's for this reason that the black people don't show their age like we do. Even in the summer they are covered, even if it's as hot as hell.

I never partook in sunbathing. Our modesty in my day was far greater than today. Covered from the bottom of the ankles to the top of the neck. There was never money for holidays, and on top of it all, so many births ruined my figure.

Most of my own daughters, and even some of their girls, have to fight the battle of the curl.

Combing hair became a wailing and gnashing of teeth.

Hair was ironed, permed, relaxed and whirled. One bottle was there to relax the curl and the other to force it into a different direction. The stuff in the tubes smells equally bad. Pure ammonia.

Where the hair comes from that frizzes so close to the scalp, makes one wonder. And shudder. And it's there that you stop wondering. They say that your hair comes from the mother's side of the family. The angry curl has been in the Van den Heever family for as long as I can remember.

The male offspring lost their mane early. The girl's scalps never saw the light of day because their hair was so thick, and the boys were balding and wore hats from an early age. Luckily a family disorder on both sides. My Joshua was as bald as the day he was born for most of the time that I knew him.

"His head is flawless," says Ester.

She examines the child from the side.

"He doesn't need hair, Ma."

I see the child through Ester's eyes.

Perfect.

That Sunday I sit contemplating the heads of my children. Because of the bald pates of the men, I suddenly notice how bumpy and gnarled our people's heads really are. We need hair to look good.

But close to the child's scalp are all the signs of a vale of tears that lie ahead.

Emily was not forgotten. Every Sunday between church and lunch, Ester and Paul took Amos and the child to Sterkfontein Hospital. With the weekly shopping she was also considered. With deodorant, soap and other feminine stuff and treats in hand, they saw her in visiting hours. Emily's head was still full of voices, but the care and pills calmed her down.

She would be allowed home for the first time after six months. Only for the weekend. Emily wasn't in a fit state to look after the child and, even then, he was brought into the house.

Raymond wasn't particularly interested in her, as he didn't know her anymore.

For any parent the child's first word is the most precious moment of contact. There is almost always a competition between both parents, hoping that the first word would be "Ma" or "Pa" (*Dad*). It's about recognition. It doesn't just happen. It comes from whispering in the ear over and over again.

"Ma," and he put his arms out. She didn't imagine it, as people generally do with any sound that these little souls make that seems familiar. It was loud and clear. Ester knew it was meant for her. She accepted it with Grace.

By the time that Raymond could think, Paul had become "Sweetheart." Paul was Ester's "Sweetheart" and now his too.

He never called Amos "Pa." Emily remained Emily

to him.

It is precisely on one such Sunday visit, months later, when Paul is so upset after church that Amos hurries away on his own to go and visit his wife.

We were always Nederduitse Gereformeerde *(Dutch Reformed)* people. The fact that all our daughters were married in the NG Church is a blessing. We didn't lose them to the other sister churches or, even worse, the Apostolic rowdiness.

It is like politics. You follow where your husband has gone before you in your name.

His Church. His politics.

This Sunday the commandments are dished up to us in a different way. The Minister starts the service in the usual manner with a reading from Matthew 22:

"And Jesus answered him: You must love the Lord your God with all your heart and all your soul, and all your mind. This is the greatest and the most important commandment. The second most important commandment goes like this: You must love your neighbour as yourself. The whole law and the teachings of the prophets depend on these two commandments."

The well-known words of the *Confessions of Faith* are mumbled without anyone giving them a second thought.

But today he goes back to the commandments and stops right there. The commandments are there to make each of us look at our own weaknesses and the harder the Minister's words hit you, the more you feel preached at by the end. Then comes the acknowledgement of our guilt.

And the Minister preaches.

"You must love your neighbour as you love yourself," he repeats out of Galatians 5 and he closes the Bible.

"The question today is: Who is my neighbour?"

I quickly recall the faces of those near to me. Family, friends and neighbours.

"It is not a political problem. It is a theological and ethical matter. It is about the transformation of our hearts," the Minister explains. "About the acceptance that we are all people, black and white, made in the image of God."

It's like with the Psalms. Old words with a new meaning.

The congregation becomes very restless.

Paul starts paging fast and furiously through his Bible, because he feels reprimanded and is looking for a different answer.

"We must open the doors. No. It shouldn't be necessary to open or close doors," persists the Minister. "There shouldn't be any doors."

With these words Ester peeps surreptitiously at her "Sweetheart," looking self-righteous, as if the sermon applies to everyone else excepting her.

"Because where there are no walls, there is also no reason to have doors."

Ester again glances at Paul.

"There must therefore be no doors or walls dividing us as Christians. In the Body of Christ we are all one."

Ester feels she is getting support from above and promptly puts Twenty Rand in the collection plate. It is an extravagant gesture, because money is always spent carefully in their home.

Under the impression of the intensity of His message, the singing of the final hymn is drawn-out with Ester singing lustily.

On the drive home the Mazda feels too small and the

road too long. I sit in front. It makes climbing in and out easier, because there is scarcely room at the back for Ester's legs.

Paul is irritable.

"Since the Dutch Reformed Church changed its tune, all we hear is politics from the pulpit."

And I get him back with something I heard on the radio.

"I told you that they say the Dutch Reformed Church is the NP praying."

But the "I told you so," doesn't work and he thunders forth.

"This *Church and Community*-manifesto of theirs is a carbon copy of the Nationalist Party's policy, which at this point isn't very different to the ANC's *Freedom Charter*."

I feel myself being drawn into a political discussion and get ready with my opinion. Admittedly, things have changed overnight. Laws are getting scrapped left, right and centre and new ideas thrown on the table. Now even the Church has changed its tune.

Like a cat who stole the cream, Ester sits with a broad smile on her face, staring out of the window without saying a word.

Paul doesn't lose his stride.

"For years they have quoted the Bible to justify *Apartheid* and now it seems they are using the same book to crucify it!"

I keep it short and sweet: "*Apartheid* was always in your Bible, not in mine."

"What do they expect from me? Do they expect me to confess and repent? Admit that *Apartheid* was a sin?" he asks belligerently. "A big mistake?" and he hits the steering wheel with a flat palm. Usually Paul is relaxed behind the wheel but today the bends are faster and feel sharper.

"The Ministers told us for years that they had sold us the only truth through the Word. And now they admit that they were wrong. It takes courage to admit that they made such a helluva mistake!"

I am also not guilt-free. My love for my neighbour was easier when everyone was white. But then the child came.

Paul doesn't let up.

"And that we are all equal!"

"Paul, did you think for one minute that when we get to heaven one day there'll be a special place for the whites, a separate place for the coloureds, and another place for the blacks?"

"And that we must all sit together in one church?!"

Paul touches a raw nerve in me, because this thing has been worrying me for years. Here I take a detour.

My Bettie's salvation was important to me. She was not given the chance to go to church on a Sunday, because there wasn't a church for them here in the white suburbs, and the inconvenience of all the children coming for lunch was the other reason.

Guilty.

But that night after the meal she was there to listen to the evening prayers. On Wednesdays after the prayer group at church, I took the Book and shared with her what I had learnt that day.

"When Jesus was here on earth to spread his message, he did it in any place, town or city. He talked to all people of any creed or colour, no matter where he was. He never stopped and said: 'Would everyone with beards and red hair go and sit and wait on that hill way over there. I'll come over and talk to you all later.'"

I don't know if Paul hears much of what I'm saying.

He silences me with: "Nowhere in the Bible am I expected to give up my own identity and to integrate to be acceptable in God's eyes, Mother."

We are coffee drinkers out of habit, but late at night and on a Sunday after church, we drink tea. We take our coffee bitter, but our tea we sweeten with a bit of sugar.

Ester is serving tea to an irritable Paul and I when the stone shatters the window right next to me.

I leap up in fright and Ester almost drops the teapot.

"He's done it again, the little scoundrel," says Ester as she storms out the house.

At the corner of the house she finds the guilty party. Throwing stones is one of Raymond's latest pastimes.

She grabs him by the arm and playfully smacks him on the bottom.

"You're costing us a fortune you little *tsotsi!*"

"Tossie," he copies her.

"You're a real little rascal. You're a *tsotsi.*"

"Tossie," once again comes out clumsily.

She *tsotsi's* him once again.

"*Tsotsi.*"

"Tossie," he lisps.

"Tossie," Ester concedes.

At that moment, he re-christens himself.

Late in the afternoon she is busy removing the last shards of glass from the flower bed and measuring the window frame for Paul. I have already been delivered, and only hear the story later.

She walks around the corner straight into Amos. She jumps momentarily as whites do at the sight of blacks.

Amos looks guilty.

"Miss Ester …" he starts with his eyes boring into the ground.

"Amos, this child of ours is sooooo naughty," she titters.

"Miss Ester …" he tries again.

"He's broken another window. It's now the third one."

"Miss Ester, it's a little girl."

Ester doesn't get it.

"Who's a little girl?"

"Emily's little girl, Miss Ester."

"What little girl?"

Ester knows he's seen Emily and is eager for news.

"Emily had a little girl."

"When?"

"Today, Miss Ester."

"Good heavens. How did that happen?"

"I don't know."

"I mean, when did you and Emily … you know …"

Ester can't get the word "sex" past her lips. It's not a word that we use. It's also not something that we talk about.

She tries as quickly as she can to turn back the calendar to work this thing out.

"I think … nine months ago."

"You mean … since she's been in hospital?"

"Must be …"

Ester is speechless.

"Or was it here?"

She shudders to think that it could have happened when they were walking around the hospital gardens with Tossie.

"My good heavens! And?"

"It's going well with her, Miss Ester. She's so beautiful," he says in a fatherly manner. "We're going to call her Mary."

"And Emily?" Ester pulls herself together.

"Emily is Emily ..."

That says it all.

"When we saw her two weeks ago, I thought she'd put on weight. She looked so good," she says to herself. "And meanwhile she was ... Paul's going to have a heart-attack."

Late that night Paul gets a phone call that is to change his path forever. It isn't so much the story itself, but the coming together of years of happenings.

He walks into the room. Ester is already in bed when he appears. Tossie is fast asleep in the bed next to her. Ester is reading her Bible. She listens with half an ear to Paul.

"I've had enough. It's the same story over and over and over ..."

"Yes," Ester agrees without actually listening.

Paul gently picks Tossie up and puts him in his own bed. He puts on his pyjamas and gets into bed.

"People have the right to know. Freedom of the press is a thing of the past ... and still ..."

Ester's silence spurs him on.

"People are scared, Ester. They just don't say it. Not aloud. But they are scared. It's ever since they abolished the Pass Laws. The blacks are everywhere. People are talking about leaving. Emigration. *'For Sale'* signs are appearing outside every second house. Young people say: 'We are doing it for the sake of our children.' Some lock up their homes and all they take is their keys in the hope that, when everything is over, they'll be able to come back. Families are disappearing in the middle of the night. Things are changing so quickly now ... I can't keep up."

Paul sounds defeated.

"The writing's on the wall, literally, there near Yeoville. The graffiti says: *'Apartheid rules.'* And someone took a can of spray paint and sprayed over the word *'Apartheid'* and changed it to the word *'Fear.'"*

He expects a reaction, but doesn't get it.

"All that you need to do to see 'Fear' in action is to drive around the streets of Johannesburg. *'Fear rules!'* It rules without a doubt. The walls are getting higher. And every second wall has a sign up that says: *'Beware! Pasop!'* In the beginning, it was broken bottles on top of the walls. Then came the barbed wire. Now it's electric fencing. The Berlin Wall is a joke compared to what we've got around our houses. These days Security is the biggest business in our country."

Ester looks at him sideways when he suddenly goes silent.

"I think I'm going to sell the newspaper."

Now he has Ester's full attention.

"Why?" She closes the Bible.

"It's enough now."

"And then?"

"And then ... I'm going to sell houses."

"It sounds like a good idea ... after what you've told me."

She switches off her bedside lamp. "Oh, before I forget," she says into the darkness. "Emily gave birth to a little girl today."

"What?"

He sits upright from shock.

"Talk more quietly," Ester whispers, "she had a baby … just now you'll wake up the child."

"They're breeding like rabbits. They're not even capable of looking after one! Not to speak of two. What is wrong with these people?" He says vehemently under his breath.

It is once again one of those things that you can make sense of after the fact. They believe – the more children, the more comfortable your old age.

I can't throw stones.

"Sleep well, my Sweetheart."

Ester turns over and closes her eyes.

We learnt an idiom at school: 'He killed a *kaffertjie*.' Which implies: It's when you can't sleep that your conscience has got to you. Paul's going to toss and turn tonight.

That Paul's story never went to print is the last straw. He suspects the reason was that it would create more panic amongst the whites.

And not without reason. Just hearing the story was enough for me.

"'Well, you see,' began Missus Smith," he recounts. "'We knew someone was siphoning petrol out of our car sometime during the day or night. It happened about three or four times. Our maid, Sanna, has worked for us for so many years that she's like a member of our family. She and the neighbour's maid caught him in the act …'"

"Mother, during the interview they stood to one side and listened to her account. While I was trying to write everything down at breakneck speed, the two maids were initially giggling and as the story progressed, they nearly laughed their heads off."

I prepared myself for to hear a story with a happy ending.

Big mistake!

"It happened yesterday morning at about eleven. In the middle of the day. Her husband was at work and she was busy in the house."

"'I didn't see anything.'"

Paul recounts it so vividly that I can almost hear her speaking.

"'As you can see, Mister, our garden is quite over-grown and that bush there was between me and the drive-way. It was then that Sanna and Flora caught the man in the act of siphoning the petrol. They confronted him. He told them to f… off and Flora, who is a large woman as you can see, saw her chance. She charged at him and, with Sanna's help, pinned him to the ground!'"

In my mind's eye I can clearly see these two large women sitting on him, almost crushing him to death, and get the urge to laugh.

"'That didn't concern me much, as you know how loud they can be,' the woman continued with her hand in front of her mouth," Paul carries on.

"'The next minute I heard this manic knocking at the front door and I heard Sanna screaming: 'Miss! Miss!' I ran to the front door. I recognised her through the fluted glass and I opened the door.'"

For a moment I relax completely. It is part of Paul's plan.

"'I got the fright of my life because she had an axe in her hand. The axe was covered in blood and so was she! For a moment I thought my time had come. I slammed the door shut because she was standing there laughing just like the two of them are laughing now,' and she gestures to the two of them. She continues: 'Through the hilarity Sanna told me that they had caught him. Who? I wanted to know, through the closed door.'"

"'"The man who's been stealing the petrol!" I heard. I put on the safety latch and opened the door ever so slightly. By then she and Flora were almost hysterical with laughter. Like now.'"

I didn't feel like laughing anymore, because this seemed to be turning ugly.

"'She said that he was lying in the driveway and that I must call the police. My first thought was that they had murdered him,' and the woman covers her mouth with her hand and shakes her head from pure terror. 'Sanna then said that I mustn't worry as he won't get away. You see, when he was first lying there, with Flora sitting on him, Sanna fetched the axe from the tool shed and she chopped both his legs off just below the knee so that he couldn't run away.'"

"Mother, and then Missus Smith dragged me to one side and whispered so that the maids couldn't hear her."

"'What I found the most frightening, Mister De Villiers, was that she thought it was funny. That's when it hit me. This woman has a key to my house. I realised then that I didn't really know her. Not this side of her.'"

"Mother, by this time she was crying so uncontrollably and between the sobs she moaned: 'You see, Mister, she looks after my children.'"

My heart shrinks and shrivels up.

"One day there's a knock at the door and, if you need a maid, you open the door freely without asking too many questions. A maid is a maid, isn't that true, Mother? It's especially working women who willingly place their most precious possession in the hands of a stranger. An almost blind trust exists on the one hand, and on the other a deep-seated fear, of the same people! The care creates a bond between the child and its black mother. I've heard stories that they even breastfeed them if it will calm the little ones down," he says without taking affront.

You do what you have to do if the situation requires it, I suddenly realise. Here at Ester and Paul the shoe is on the other foot.

Paul qualifies as an Estate Agent at the grand age of seventy-two after selling the newspaper. The fact that he now works from home, makes everyone's lives a bit easier, especially when it comes to babysitting.

The week after Mary's birth they go to see it. Paul with a doll in his hand.

Emily is aware of Mary, but isn't quite with the picture. Who could blame her when everything of this world has become a blur to her?

After six months, according to hospital policy, a plan has to be made with the little girl.

"I suppose she should also come to us then," were the words that came out of Paul's mouth that sounded like a miracle.

And suddenly there were two. Everything that was pink got carried into the house. Paul was also strangely enough the one who couldn't get enough of Mary.

A cot was carried into the adjoining room, and it didn't matter what time of the day or night it was, if there was the tiniest noise, it was Paul who flew out of bed to go and check.

With Tossie almost three, he becomes Paul's right-hand man with the hammering in and taking out of the *"For Sale"* signs, while Mary goes along everywhere on the backseat for a ride.

Mary is with them for eight months or so when he comes home one afternoon and finds Amos there with the unknown woman.

When he stops, Tossie jumps out of the car and runs right past Amos, and straight into the house.

Paul meets them, holding Mary in his arms.

"I am Missus Green," she introduces herself in English. "I am the social worker from the Sterkfontein Institution for the Mentally Handicapped."

"De Villiers. Pleased to meet you ... I hope." He reciprocates in his perfect English. He could speak it as he could write it. "Is there a problem that I can help you with?"

Amos doesn't look happy and that makes Paul feel uncomfortable.

"Has something happened to Emily? We saw her last Sunday and she looked fine. We always take her the necessities ..."

"Emily isn't the problem," she interrupts him. "Under the circumstances, things are going well."

"Thank God," says Paul. He looks up to the heavens and means it.

"It's the children. They are the problem."

"Master Paul, I have tried to explain to her."

"Let her finish."

And she bombards him.

"Seeing that Emily will need to stay in the institution for an indeterminate length of time, and because of the fact that she can't even take care of herself, let alone the little ones, and because Amos here has a fulltime job, during the day I mean, we need to find another solution. We need to do what is best for the children."

"So far we're not doing too badly," Paul tries to defend.

"Mister De Villiers, I mean this with the greatest respect, but neither you nor your wife can be held responsible for the welfare of the children. I am sure your contribution is greatly appreciated but, even if they were white, you wouldn't qualify as foster parents. You and your wife are a bit long in the tooth."

"Maybe true in my case, but my wife ..."

"How old are you, Mister De Villiers?"

"I'll be seventy two this month. My wife has just turned fifty."

She frowns as she stands doing sums in her head.

"So young," she thinks aloud. "Anyway, research has proved that it is seldom in the child's best interest to be brought up outside of its own culture. And especially in this country of all countries something like this is impossible."

By this time Paul is annoyed.

"Look, I have listened to you patiently and I know you are only doing your job. But isn't there something that you are missing here?"

"Like what?"

"Not what? Who? Why do you keep acting as if the child's father isn't here? As if he doesn't have a say in it. He can talk for himself, you know. Have you asked him what he would like? They are his children too."

"Well, Master, I have tried to explain, but it seems as if she doesn't understand. According to our way, Mary will have to go to her Ouma."

"Oh no, not to Patricia," says a despondent Paul. "The Father preserve us. Not after what she did!"

"You see!" snaps Missus Green.

"Keep quiet until he's finished!" Paul loses his patience, knowing that she doesn't have the faintest idea of what all this is about.

"No, my Old Master," Amos gets the chance to explain his story. "To Emily's mother, Evelina, in Chrissiesmeer. But what this woman doesn't understand is that Tossie must stay. Tossie is not Emily's child. He is Miss Ester's child."

There is one of those family get-togethers two Sundays later to celebrate Paul's birthday. Betta and Baby are alone in the kitchen making salad.

I had plugged my transistor-radio in in the kitchen earlier. When I hear the signature tune of the one-o'clock news I move closer. This week the radio is chockablok with another birthday party that the government vehemently intended to put a stop to. The birthday of Mandela, who turns seventy today.

On the same day, but two years younger than Paul. Can you believe it? I want to hear the conclusion of the case, but what I hear and see in Ester's kitchen completely overshadows the day's news.

The two are staring out of the window watching Ester who is playfully chasing the children with a dishcloth in her hand. The two of them are so busy that they don't see me coming.

"It's become impossible to invite them anywhere," I hear one of my daughters say. I had suspected that the family had been talking like this amongst themselves.

Betta is chopping the onions with serious intent.

"It shames me to death!"

"It's bad enough coming here," says Baby. "And then to stand face to face with them going so crazy about the child!" She arranges the slices of tomato around the edge of the dish.

"They have no respect for other people's feelings!"

"Do you know how I felt the other day when I bumped into them in Westgate? I went shopping with a friend and the next moment … there they stood. Black child and all. I wished the earth would swallow me up."

"What is wrong with them?" Betta asks through her veil of onion tears.

"But what amazes me is that Paul is so outspoken these days about the blacks. He doesn't want them in the same church, or in schools, not to mention as neighbours! And on the other hand they're nurturing this one as their own. Then suddenly his colour doesn't matter. And all that you hear out of his mouth these days is … what does he call it again?" asks Baby.

"His 'conservative beliefs and values,'" Betta helps her out and breaks the onion pieces into separate rings.

"How do you explain this to someone?" Baby wants to know while gesturing with the knife towards outside.

Ester chases the children right around the Blue Gum trees.

"My grandchildren don't want to come here anymore either, because they're scared that they'll be forced to play with the *kaffertjie*.

It is only when the little children swarm through the kitchen into the dining room with Ester in hot pursuit that the two of them see me for the first time.

Suddenly Baby is very busy with the pepper and the vinegar, hurriedly pouring it over the tomatoes, and Betta yanks open the oven door pretending to check whether the sugar on the pumpkin has melted yet.

"How long have you been here, Ma?" Baby asks.

I don't want them to know that I have overheard the whole conversation and hurriedly say something about the last part.

"Have you forgotten how you played with the black kids on the farm, Betta, when you were a child? And you, Baby? You and the black klonkies (*piccaninnies*) were always inseparable."

Just then Ester returns, laughing and out of breath.

"But then it was considered normal," Betta defends herself.

"They were the only other children in the area for miles," says Baby, as if that would make a difference.

"Then they were good enough," I remind them.

"What are you talking about?" Ester wants to know.

"I am just reminding your sisters of how they used to play with black children on the farm. It seems that they've forgotten."

A second later we are overrun with children.

Tossie is plucking and pulling at Ester's sleeve.

"Ma, Ma, when can we have cake?" And that in perfect Afrikaans too. "Ah, please."

"Later. You children must stop running through the

house. You must play outside," and this coming from Ester, the ringleader.

With screams and yells they rush out of the house.

"That was great fun!" There is a certain sentiment in the way that Ester says this.

Betta and Baby each grab a bowl with salad and get out as fast as they can. As they pass, Betta whispers to Baby, as if she thinks I'm deaf: "It looks to me he thinks he's an Afrikaans boy and that he's white!"

"And then one day we had to stop that," Ester says almost to herself. "I could never understand why."

I understood why and helped to put a stop to it. How could it be any different? My girls were busy budding and the black boys becoming randy. I saw my own sons come into the rutting season and it was also a problem there. You don't look for trouble where trouble doesn't exist. It is there in black and white in the law.

"They came to take her away on Friday," Ester says with great pain. "You know, Ma, if Paul had had a choice, it would have been Tossie."

"I know that, my child."

"Ma, I've never seen him like that before. It was almost as bad as a death," and she takes the plates out of the warm drawer. "He really loves her. She's the apple of his eye."

The pain in his eyes was obvious this morning when I wished him and gave him my unassuming present. Handkerchiefs for Christmas and a tie for birthdays. He wore it to church today. Bluish with grey and maroon stripes.

"It broke his heart. He barely had time to say goodbye. I think the social worker had been the hell in with him since the first time she came here. She apparently jumped in the car, slammed the door, opened her window and asked him: 'Whose side are you actually on anyway?' and sped off. All that he wanted was for Amos to say his say. And what he then said didn't suit her at all. Paul isn't perfect, Ma. But no-one can ever say: Paul de Villiers doesn't play fair."

Little does she know? I become immersed in thought about my two sons, Sarel and Gert's conversation earlier around the fire.

"You'd think," said Gert, opening a beer and pouring a bit over the meat, because it gives it a delicious flavour, "that with his journalistic background he would rather have chosen liberal politics, like the Progressive Party. After all he worked for *The Star*. He told me the other day, that with things as they are at John Vorster Square, the blacks feel safer telling their stories to *The Star* than to the police. And now this!"

The thing about Paul and the English, along with the newspaper, gives you an idea of his determination. Apparently his teacher at school told him that whatever he chose to do with his future he should rather do it in Afrikaans, because with his rotten English he would never succeed.

"To struggle for so many years. Working fulltime and studying part-time. Towards an MBA," says Gert. "From the most junior of junior journalists to the president of the Council of Journalists. And to now take it all and throw it away like that, because of the Conservative Party! I can't understand it!"

"What's right is right. He's a man of principle, Ma," Ester says on her way to the table while she helps me down the stairs.

"For him a principle is a principle," Ester starts and I join in with the rhyme that we know so well.

"A principle is a principle."

"Irrefutably!" I reply triumphantly.

"Like the laws of the Medes and the Persians!" Ester finishes it off.

And we laugh till our sides ache.

The feast begins.

Paul sits at the head of the table. Tossie sits on his lap. Sarel proposes a toast.

"Long may he live, long may he live in his glory ..." We sing to him as if at a wedding.

"To Paul," and Sarel raises his glass.

"To Paul," and everyone clinks glasses.

"And here's to his twin brother, Nelson, who could unfortunately not be here today."

Everyone laughs. Knowingly.

Without batting an eyelid Paul acknowledges the toast with: "And may he rot in jail."

He hugs Tossie and kisses him on the forehead and takes a big sip of champagne.

Paul, Ester and Tossie are on their way to the Westgate Shopping Centre, in the green Mazda 323. I usually avoid the Shopping Centres, especially Westgate, because all the walking is too much for me.

Paul drives. He looks up and catches Tossie's eye in the rear-view mirror.

Paul begins with: "When we're at home, who is Ester?"

Tossie is rather bored with the game.

"Ma," he says drily.

"And when we go to Westgate Shopping Centre?"

"Miss Ester."

"Good, and when we get home what do you call me?"

"Sweetheart."

"And at Westgate?"

"Pa," he says wilfully.

Ester starts giggling.

Paul usually finds this quick-wittedness in the child endearing, but this isn't the time or place.

"No! I am?" he asks again.

"Master Paul."

"Nice." And Paul is satisfied.

"Nice," repeats Ester. "This is a 'nice' photo of you."

Ester refers to the rows of Municipal Election Posters on the lampposts on both sides of Ontdekkers Road. They say:

"Paul de Villiers, Conservative Party Candidate, Ward 3."

That Paul liked the Conservatives was also explainable. Their way of thinking was acceptable to him. It was all about "old" values. The "old" values that had kept South Africa white. He denies that their leadership is based on race in any way and justifies it with: "*Apartheid* makes everyone separate but equal." Paul's view is that he doesn't think he is better than anyone else, just different.

Actually they are exactly the same as the National Party were before they changed their tune.

Paul's problem with the NP is that he couldn't see where they were heading. They change things and abolish laws left, right and centre without putting something acceptable in its place.

As the oldest he feels he needs to spell it out to me.

"People feel unsafe and that they don't have a vision of the future to believe in anymore. That's why the young ones are leaving and the older ones have started dabbling in the stock exchange. It's the bottom of the social and money ladder that worries me. The working class. If they take away all our privileges, those that already have so little are left with nothing. I can't stand and watch our people sinking back all the way to where we came from," he says, sighing, emptying his lungs. "People with money can afford to be liberal. The only freedom we'll ever have is to overcome poverty. And we've done this in a big way, but now Botha wants to give it all away."

I think: But you are the people who voted him in and now you're moaning!

Baby and a friend, each with a trolley, are shopping at Pick 'n Pay. Her friend's son, a young boy of maybe thirteen, has a strange hairstyle. Shaved bald at the sides and the rest standing up dead straight on top. He's also wearing a bunch of cheap gold chains around his neck. He looks rather strange for his age.

The next minute Baby spots Ester with Tossie in the trolley.

"Ooh, I forgot to get washing powder," she says, making up a story.

She turns on her tail, ducks behind a display of tinned foods and disappears in the opposite direction to where Ester is coming from.

"Miss Ester, could I have a Tinkie," Tossie asks when they get to the aisle with the sweets.

"With pleasure, Master Tossie!"

Ester hates this routine, but joins in to save Paul embarrassment when out and about. She stops at the Tinkies and throws a handful into the trolley.

On the way in Paul spots one of his committee members, a National Party man with the surname Treleven, and waits for him.

Ester and Tossie quickly make tracks.

Although the people here in the west of Johannesburg are predominantly Afrikaans, Roodepoort is a National Party seat.

Treleven is the one in control of rates and taxes and Paul has a bone to pick with him.

"You and your government are selling our birth right for a bowl of lentil stew," Paul jumps in in his best English.

"If the NP wins this election, we might as well give the blacks everything now."

"For a change we are doing what is right for all the people of Roodepoort," Treleven puts him in his place.

Paul doesn't just fall for that.

"You of all people should know what's going to happen with our taxes and stuff, the day we incorporate Dobsonville into the greater Roodepoort! Tax will go through the roof and services will collapse completely. You can't incorporate the Third World without permanently damaging the First World standards. We've worked hard to get things to this point ..."

"At the expense of cheap black labour," Treleven completes his sentence for him.

Treleven gets interrupted by an excited black child running towards them. He grabs Paul's hand and starts pulling.

"Sweetheart, hurry up, Ma is standing and waiting," he says while tugging at Paul's hand.

"Tossie, can't you see I'm busy talking?" He reprimands the child.

Just then Ester rounds the corner with far too much shopping. Tossie sees her and turns and runs to her.

"Ma. Ma. Sweetheart says he's busy talking."

At that precise moment two women walk past Paul. "And I said to the maid, if you can't talk Afrikaans, then find me someone who can!" The one says to the other.

"And rightly so," the other one agrees.

Without batting an eyelid Paul says: "He's our maid's child. He calls all women 'Ma.'"

Ester smiles to herself and looks at Paul. Paul in his turn looks at Treleven, whilst Treleven also in turn stares at the two women. He shakes his head.

Somewhere in the parking lot a car alarm is going off. People suddenly seem to move a little faster.

It's a Saturday night and just after the news it's the *A-Team*. Tossie is sitting on the carpet in front of the TV.

Paul is busy doing a crossword puzzle and I am crocheting.

When Tossie screams: "Hit him, hit him," I look up. On the screen there is a huge muscular black man knocking the living daylights out of a white man. On his head is the renowned hairstyle. Shaved at the sides and a cock's-comb on top. A bunch of chains hangs around his neck.

Like Paul's Drakensberger they are everywhere on the TV these days. Amongst the whites just like that. And it riles him.

"You see, Mother, this is how these things affect

mostly the children. Soon they won't be able to differentiate. They are going to start thinking that this is how it should be. Whites and blacks together. It's a conspiracy by the government, these goings on."

I looked first at Paul and then at Tossie.

"It looks to me like its working!" and I can see that Paul is annoyed by my words.

The BA-Baracus-character is everyone's hero.

Ester walks in with a tray. Paul stands up to take it from her.

"I can manage it myself, thank you," she says gently because she doesn't mean to be rude.

Pauls stands around helplessly for a moment. I feel a bit sorry for him, because Ester is undermining his manhood. Not literally. She's depriving him of his pride and manly duties.

Ester puts the tray down on the coffee table. She walks over to where I'm sitting and almost automatically switches on the standing lamp behind me.

"Ma, you mustn't sit in the dark and work, it's bad for your eyes."

Ester goes and sits down again.

"Tossie, turn the TV down. I can't hear myself think," says Paul.

Ester just rolls her eyes.

"And who are you crocheting for this time, Ma?"

"Martie's little one."

Ester puts a cup of tea on the side table for me and offers me biscuits.

"Ma, you must stop this some or other time. It's enough for one lifetime. You've must have made at least a hundred!"

"I'll stop on the day … it's seventy-eight … that my family stops breeding. Or on the day that you carry me to my grave. An Ouma must do what she must do. My eyes get tired … especially at night … it's the dark wool."

"Paul," Ester asks, pouring his tea. "What has happened to people? Wherever you go Afrikaners insist on being served in Afrikaans. A woman caused such a fuss the other day. I was so embarrassed. She went on and on: 'Call the manageress then.' And I turned to her and asked her: What if the manageress is black? It's possible, you know. Would you be able to talk to her in her language?"

Ester hands Paul his tea.

"Ester, what do you think the riots ever since the sixty's were about? The blacks refuse to learn Afrikaans."

"They say it's the language of the oppressor!" I butt in.

Both Ester and Paul stare at me for a brief second as if I've gone mad.

"They said so on the radio."

"And now they're scared that things are going to change so much in the future that you won't be able to speak Afrikaans wherever you want to." Paul's voice sounds almost teary.

"In my time when everything became English, and you spoke Afrikaans, they put donkey-ears on your head and forced you to sit in the corner," I said dryly. "If the Afrikaners had taken to the streets and revolted like the blacks are doing today, it could have been another story. But no! All that they did was give up! And sit around and moan. Nobody then insisted on being served in a shop in Afrikaans. Not in the schools. Not even in church. Everyone then thought English was so grand. You would think that after the concentration camps they would never have wanted to hear that sound in their ears again. But our people couldn't wait!" I say without missing a stitch.

Six months later Paul attaches the *"For-Sale"* sign to the gate of the plot. He feels that the market is buoyant and says that there is talk that shops are going to be built here. Their neighbours sold on a whim and he feels it is time to live amongst his voters.

He won Ward Three for the KP.

Sarel's plot had been sold months ago. Paul got him a good price.

Animals are slaughtered and the pig pen is filled in. By this time there are only five or six of the yapping Toypoms left. As they died, Ester no longer kept a pup from each litter as she'd done before.

Paul catches a pigeon sitting on the edge of an empty cage.

"This one keeps coming back," Paul says almost despairingly. As if he doesn't know that coming back is in their nature.

"This is a bad day," is Amos' bad tiding. "There's not a cow left to milk, the sheep are all gone … and all the chickens are in the deep-freeze. What are we going to do now, my Master?"

"I know it's not much, but at least the house is new, and you've still got a roof over your head. I've already spoken to someone from our church. He's got work for you. Because, other than the lawn mowing and the flower beds, there's not much for you to do. You can start on Monday already," Paul consoles him in a fatherly manner.

Paul releases the pigeon up into the air.

It flies away.

Tossie runs from room to room looking for Ester.

"Ma, Ma!" he shouts at the top of his lungs, so that it echoes through the empty rooms.

He finds her in the bathroom perched on the edge of the bath. She quickly wipes her eyes so that he can't see that she's been sitting and crying.

The move is the one reason. She was happy here. The fact that we are taking the road towards Dobsonville with Sarel the next day is the other.

Now, of the sons, there is just Gert left. The clods on my daughter, Marina's grave are still fresh.

It is an early service so that those who need to get back to work aren't too late. It is the middle of the week and Ester had already taken time off to pack when Sarel eventually succumbed to the cancer. He suffered so terribly and for so long, my poor child, that there was almost nothing left of him.

Ester's flowers on the coffin and in the church are beautiful. The vibrant yellow of the Chrysanthemums can't put the sun back in my heart. I am too dark and empty inside.

The Minister speaks well of him, as they are wont to do on occasions like these. Luckily he had known Sarel. He doesn't need to exaggerate. There is, in all honesty, nothing bad to say about him.

At around ten o'clock the funeral procession makes its way through Roodepoort at a respectful pace. The police, riding on motorbikes up ahead to control the approaching traffic, leave us to our own devices at the large traffic circle where we cross Main Reef Road, because all that is left is a long empty stretch of road to Sarel's final resting place.

Ester and Marieke are together in the family car and Baby with me and Paul, because her husband couldn't get off work.

We are fifth in line in the funeral procession, or we would have seen it sooner.

First the hearse and then car after car get swallowed up by the blackness. Had we been paying attention, we would have heard the crowd of protestors with their knopkieries *(clubs)* and their banners.

Inside the car the darkness engulfs us. Only a few darkly press their faces against the windows. Others bang on the roof of the car.

Marieke doesn't even look up. She is resting her head on Ester's shoulder.

Ester doesn't move a muscle. She looks them straight in the eye.

Baby, who is sitting behind me, makes a squeal like a tiny piglet and clasps her mouth. As surreptitiously as possible she locks the door of the car with her elbow.

Paul looks straight ahead. His blue eyes are like slits. The corners of his mouth that are turned down to his shoulders are the only sign of his displeasure. The beads of sweat on his forehead could have been from the heat. We are in the heart of summer and it had been sweltering since eight o'clock, which is why we had decided to get this miserable happening behind us early.

I am too heart sore to feel faint. My feeling is: what will be, will be.

All that they left behind them was a fingerprint or two.

Nothing happened.

Black people have respect for the dead. Bettie once told me that they are bonded to their ancestors.

All that Paul has to say about it, after we've had tea and cake at the church hall, once it is all over is: "You see, Mother."

What I was supposed to see, I don't know. I saw what I saw. They didn't have an issue with us.

As flat as the land had been at the plot, this new place is in the hills. The front yard is far, far down there and the back twice as high as the roof. The steepness doesn't bother me. Luckily the driveway takes you right to the front door.

There isn't a gate or a fence to speak of at the front. Their house almost looks out of place in this area, where a person can determine the age of the walls, like the rings in the trunk of a tree, from the different colour-shades of the cement between the bricks. A little higher and higher every year until only the roofs are visible.

The back garden is God's own rockery. There is rock wherever you look. You can't easily dig anywhere here. How they dug the swimming pool beats me, but it was one of the main reasons they bought this place. No matter where you sit on the back *stoep* – a long wide one – you are below the bottom of the swimming pool. This becomes our place to sit and relax instead of the old Loquat tree.

Everybody who could make it is here to christen the new house. It is Saturday, otherwise nobody would have swum. The no-swimming-on-a-Sunday law was quickly laid down. As with our sewing, it is not allowed. It is the Day of Rest and must be respected as such.

Out of the blue, a child jumps into the swimming pool, splashing all the other children sitting on the sides and drenching all of us below.

"Stop it," one shouts.

It is Tossie who made a water bomb.

Gawie, one of my great-grandchildren, runs dripping wet to his mother, Annelien.

"Ma, Ma," he shouts. "Look, the little baboon can swim."

Had it been anyone else's child he might have got away with it, and been laughed at for doing it. Annelien grabs his arm and gives him a helluva hiding. It is still the good old days where a flat hand is used when necessary.

"Don't you ever say that again," hitting him soundly between the "ever" and the "again." "Do you understand me?"

The child wails while leaping into the air.

My grandchildren already have a completely different mindset to my own children. Especially the few who have been to University.

Baby and Betta are also sitting on the stoep. They of course start to giggle.

I hang my head in shame.

"What made you decide to buy here? I know it's a much better suburb, but it's so ... English," Gert wants to know.

"They voted me in. This is my ward," is Paul's logical retort.

It is, ironically enough. The area is predominantly English and is full of young couples who are just starting families. I look at Ester long and hard when she says: "Ma, I feel completely at home here," and I know she isn't talking about speaking English.

"I never knew there were so many English-speaking KP's in Roodepoort," Gert says rather amazed.

"Why not?" Paul half-questions. "They are young and well-off and they also deserve peace of mind. And what's more, I speak their language. None of the liberal parties could ever make the grade amongst the English. Not here. Neither in Greenside or Houghton. They are also in the greatest majority there. With the biggest bank accounts. And the biggest mouths. And unfortunately, not a single seat," he says victoriously. "In this last election we proved it. We threw sand in the liberal's eyes and became the official opposition. Forty percent of the whites are English. With our own people being so headstrong, they should have made a difference. But no. Until now they have never shown much interest in politics, because they were economically empowered compared to our people who had to fight for our preservation. All that I'm doing now is using the KP to build a bridge between the English and Afrikaner. At last!"

I want to laugh about this, because he is sounding like a typical SAP.

"Two parts of one whole. The liberals will never admit it. It looks to me like they understand the situation through my eyes."

When Paul talks like this it is easy to keep quiet and listen.

"Because, you see, we're all scared now. Fear talks a common language. And that brings us together."

"I meant that I thought most of the English had already left the country by now," jokes Gert.

And they all laugh heartily.

Ester is busy showing Marieke and Grieta, her and Sarel's daughter, the house. Marieke is appropriately dressed in the required black.

This house is also four-bedroomed, but this time with a second bathroom. My room, if I can call it that, is directly opposite one of them. Almost nothing has changed for me, excepting that the distance to the kitchen is shorter.

"Sarel would have loved this house," Marieke says, still deeply affected by her loss.

When she starts crying, Ester is there to comfort her.

"He was a good man. He helped us so much with Tossie. Ah, Marieke, it's for the best."

We always say "It's for the best" when someone has suffered. Death brings an end to the suffering, but these words seldom give comfort to the one left behind. But it is fitting.

Grieta comes out of one of the rooms lower down the passage.

"Whose room is this?" she says perplexed.

"Tossie's."

"Oh ..." and her eyes are out on stalks.

Grieta looks back into the bedroom. It's the perfect room for a boy. Everything is kitted out in blue. Hanging above the bed is a gigantic poster of a man wearing spectacles and a severe expression. At the top reads: *"AP Treurnicht – KP"* and at the bottom *"Our Leader."*

On Sunday, the following day, we get dressed early. Tossie is nearly four by now, and his salvation needs to be assured. The earlier you drag the little ones to Church, the quicker they learn to sit still through the long services.

When my children were his age and got ants in their

pants, I had my own means of calming them down. To keep on with "Shhhh, Shhhh!" throughout the service left you sounding like a punctured inner tube. And it was disruptive. I had my ammunition in my handbag. I firstly opened the flask with the golden syrup and rubbed it onto their hands just with my finger. Before they had a chance to lick their fingers, I quickly gave them a ball of cotton-wool. For the next hour and a quarter or so they struggled to get the cotton-wool off their hands. The more they tried, the more it stuck. Later on it started forming long threads. Just before the collection, I took out a wet face-cloth and rescued them.

Ester is busy doing Tossie's tie. He is dressed for Church. In his shorts, jacket and white shirt he looks priceless.

Boys only start wearing long pants when they are about twelve. They look forward to it for years, because it means that they are now grown up. The shoes are polished the night before. The long grey socks first get pulled up over the knees and then turned over. With the socks nowadays it isn't necessary to use elastics to hold them up.

"Promise me that you'll sit still and be quiet," Ester gives instructions like a real mother. She stands back and examines him from head to toe. "Lovely," she nods her approval.

He stretches out his "Yes, Ma" out of boredom because she has been fussing over him like a hen with her chickens.

The doorbell rings.

"That's probably Tonia," says Ester.

Tonia and her Dutch husband are their next-door-neighbours. At one point they frowned on Ester, Paul and the child, but they very soon became attached to the De Villiers' with their little black son. Their little Peter is Tossie's age and they soon became playmates. At that age it isn't necessary to understand one another, as long as you have fun playing together. They have their own sign language. Tossie could soon "Yes" and "No" like I could. And it stayed like that just as it did with me.

He wants to rush out the door, but Ester holds him back by the arm. She hasn't finished her story. She shoves a ten cent piece into his hand.

"It's not for sweets. When the collection plate comes round, then you put it in, do you hear?" she explains to him.

He "Yes, Ma's" her and runs ahead to the front door.

I was by now sitting ready and waiting on the bench in the entrance hall. I sit and watch him as he stretches on tiptoes to turn the door handle, and feel as if I'm getting a preview of how he will look in his school uniform one day. My chest swells with pride.

Ester and Paul are bringing him up well.

I shuffle to the car ahead of them. Paul catches up with me at the top of the two steps on the *stoep* and offers me his arm to help me down. There are only two to get down here as compared to the seven at the other house. Paul holds the door open for me with one hand, too scared to let me go, because if I topple over it'll take more than him and Ester to get me back on my feet again.

Opening the door for a woman has been drummed into the men's heads from an early age.

Ester climbs in with my Church hat in her hand. And we drive off.

Ester, like most of the young people, hasn't worn a hat in years. It is only the oldies like me who feel half-naked without one. Ester keeps it on her lap until we get to Church, so that it doesn't mess up my hair unnecessarily. After we get out, it gets handed over and I put it on and check if it's sitting straight in the reflection from the window.

As proud as I feel on one hand, I am as irritable as anything on the other and I start up with: "What is the sense in sending him with Tonia and them. You feel he should go to church to be saved, but it's all in English. Yes, it's all good and well that he goes, but he won't understand a word of it."

Paul keeps dead quiet.

"Ma, you know how things are in the Afrikaans Churches when it comes to blacks," Ester says, as if it's new to me, and she glances sideways at Paul.

The car stops outside the Dutch Reformed Church. Paul gets out quickly, opens my door and helps me out.

Ester opens her window.

"Ma, we'll fetch you in about two hours," she says without getting out of the car.

When I find my feet and have checked my hat on my head, I reproach her.

"Your father and I didn't bring you up like this, my child."

She doesn't argue. She just says it as it is.

"You did. You taught me that I should go to my husband's Church and become a member of his political party. I don't have a choice," she says softly. But clearly. It was also meant for Paul's ears.

"Wait for us on that bench, if we're a little late."

They drive off.

And I think to myself: This is how this country's politics affects our family. It also tears us apart.

As with politics, Paul wants the Church to remain as it is. As with the KP, the Afrikaanse Protestantse Kerk *(Afrikaans Protestant Church)* is familiar to him.

Paul helped establish this congregation which at that time was served from a school hall. The building of their church would still take months.

Their Minister, Christo Fourie, preaches about the APK standpoint in a way that suites Paul's point of view of "different, but not better."

"We, the Afrikaans Protestant Church for White Afrikaners, make allowances for the Unity of the Body of Christ. But also make provision for the diversity as written in John 10: v16. The book of John says:

There are other sheep that belong to me that are not in this sheep pen. I must bring them too; they will listen to my voice and they will become one flock with one shepherd."

Paul is all ears. These words sound like music to him.

"We are not blind to the suffering of other people. We have compassion however for the spiritual welfare of our own flock. The Afrikaner."

Paul adjusts his position and sits with a broad smile on his face.

"And today," Minister Fourie concludes, "when you make your offerings to the Lord, think about it this way: I give my offering to build a church for my people. I give my offering to build a house for the Lord!"

For years the NG Church has been renowned for its incessant money collection, and now the APK are doing the same. And Paul feels even more at home.

In the same way that the congregation's singing – accompanied by a piano – has lost its way, so does the church choir.

It is during the collection and singing of the choir that Ester looks up for the first time. Ester has stared at her shoes throughout the service to keep her thoughts elsewhere. Not that Ester can sing at all, but she can hear that a disservice is being done to: *"The Lord is My Shepherd."*

By this time the plate has reached Paul. He places a large pink note in the plate and hands it to Ester while watching her closely. Without a gesture she gives it to the woman next to her.

Paul just shakes his head.

After the service Paul gets chatting, but Ester is in a hurry. She just wants to leave. While Paul is talking to Bertie Nagel, she is waiting in the car. Bertie's wife is serving tea along with the other women, or this conversation would have had to wait till later.

It is already heating up and Ester only hears the end of it through the car window.

"I mean," she hears Paul say, "Amos has been working for you for a few months or so, and we've known him for many years and, as you yourself know, he is very trustworthy. I am aware it's just a shack, but I will fix it up myself. We'll put in new windows and a door. At our own expense."

"It's so typical of the blacks," says Bertie and Ester pricks up her ears. "Can you believe it? Last week they carried off two windows and nine bags of cement. Not to mention the untold fortune of bricks and ..."

Paul has heard it all before and interrupts him.

"At least in the day there's a white supervisor to keep an eye on them. But at night there's nobody. The church stands alone and unprotected. That's why I think that…"

"… Amos should look after a church that he will never be allowed to enter," Ester completes his sentence.

Bertie glares at Ester with a scowl on his face. His wife would never dare to say something like that.

Paul paces uncomfortably. She had said it to him before when he had discussed it with her, but he would have preferred it had she not repeated it here.

These days there is a stubbornness in her that wasn't there before.

But she carries on: "They are good enough to build the church and to look after it …"

And Bertie silences Ester as if she is his own wife.

"But Missus De Villiers," he keeps it civil, "they're not stealing from us, they're stealing from God!"

Ester rolls her eyes and shuts the window.

With less work to do in the garden and his work at the Bertie-character's business, Amos comes home less at night and smells more often of drink. It worries Ester.

"If he was here at least now and then, then we could keep an eye on him," she urges Paul. "If we leave him to seal his own fate at the church grounds, I don't know what's going to become of him. We must rather find good reasons to bring him home. The child isn't enough anymore."

She turns on the car radio. She channel-hops to find something to listen to that will drown out the voices of Paul and Bertie.

As he gets into the car; she tunes into the half-hour news on *Radio Highveld*.

"Mister De Klerk announced," reads Helen Naudé, "that one of the first bottlenecks that he wants to address is the unbanning of political parties and the release of prominent political prisoners." Ester intentionally turns the sound up. "Since his appointment as State President he has not only had praises heaped on him abroad, but here in the very corridors of the Union Buildings ..." and Paul switches the radio off.

What we didn't hear at home about Paul's political antics, we read about in the *Roodepoort Herald*. There was hardly an issue where they didn't quote him on what he got up to during political meetings. And in the next copy you could expect a reply from him in the letter section. Always in English. At the meetings everything was in English for the sake of the English. That's the reason they also quoted his addresses in English.

If you want to get Paul firing on all six cylinders, you only need to mention what could possibly happen to education in this country in the future.

I have half read and half heard this story. And it is because it is in English that I only half understand it, because with his way with words it goes right over my head.

He had done his homework about issues like this as one would expect of the journalist he had been before. Thoroughly. And you are inclined to believe him because of this.

Ester can speak English well enough to make it easily understandable and she explains the front page article to me.

"You see, Ma, they did some or other study in America about the past thirty years of enforced integration in their schools."

This interests her because, before you know it, Tossie

will be ready for school and what then?

"Paul is referring here to the conclusions of a Doctor Garrett about the problems that have arisen in mixed schools in America and that it only leaves a few options open for the school governing body," she says, translating the article almost word for word.

I've got to listen carefully and think hard to digest it all.

"You have to lower the standards for the Negroes to keep up, at the expense of the whites who can no longer develop their full potential." She reads the next part to herself and then comes back with: "Either you adjust it to suit the whites, in which case the Negroes will fail or drop out, which will in turn lead to problems requiring special attention. In both cases you undermine the strength of the education system."

She drops the newspaper into her lap like someone whose arms have gone lame. Ester ponders on it a bit more, before she gathers the strength to read further. "If you already mix the two in first grade, you suddenly sit with a Negro culture. Both cultures adopt the worst qualities of the other very quickly. And, Ma, then he refers here to bad habits, customs, moral standards, attitudes, and very quickly it works its way down to their use of language," she quotes him again.

Ester flings the newspaper onto the ground and storms out the door. I thought that this was where the story would end.

There is a bit of truth in the last part, because we have seen for ourselves how quickly the blacks ape the whites when it comes to our weaknesses.

But she suddenly appears again, and picks up where

she left off.

"Thirdly he stands by his belief that 'integration' and 'quality' are not compatible. Then he quotes his own mother who always said that regret is a good thing, but that regret always comes too late. And he ends with the words: 'Be warned!' Then they refer here to the NP members who apparently also warned him in their turn with P.W Botha's words: *'Adapt or Die.'*" And for a brief moment she seems more content.

In the beginning Botha was everyone's hero, because anyone who could speak like that was a president close to your heart.

"Our people," Paul poured his heart out when I quite innocently asked him about the *'Adapt or Die'* thing, "have always had a mutual respect for and fear of their leaders and PW can intimidate both black and white in this manner."

Botha had had his turn at instilling fear in everyone. The more scared they were, the more subservient.

"And then he came with his reform plans and intimidated us and forced us to choose. And then the right thinkers and I moved."

"Right-wingers," I correct him. "As he opened the sluices, he tried to divert the wall of water, because he knew the flood couldn't be stopped," I remind him.

"Conceded," says Paul and I am amazed at him, because concessions within politics are not something Paul makes easily. "He gathered his generals and police force around him and declared the country in a State of Emergency. He didn't have a choice. But under him the violence escalated and escalated. And then, after all the years of creating chaos, he resigned. If it wasn't for the pressure from the British and the Americans, we would still be saddled with him. His hands are not too clean, Mother. But with this new one, we are going to slide into a bloodbath!"

With the arrival of De Klerk, the face of politics changed. Gone was the one with the skew mouth and the pointing finger. Now we have another bald one, but this one talks more quietly and has a boyish smile.

He's got a nice head, I think to myself.

But he isn't the only new face that we have to get used to. On the one front there is Mandela and on the other the man on horseback, Eugene Terre'Blanche, with the blue eyes and roaring voice, who is turning more and more heads. De Klerk is a man of his word and Mandela gets released after twenty seven years.

On the day of his release we are glued to the TV. We watch with bated breath as they throw open the prison doors. And nothing happens. His wife, Winnie, comes out and says that he is going to sit it out until they bring the State of Emergency to an end.

"Mother, do you see how he's taunting us," Paul says in disgust.

The day that he agrees to come out, I'm not sure which one he actually is, because his face has been hidden from us for so many years.

"Paul," Ester asks. "Is it the one walking with the Winnie-woman?"

And there he stands. The face of the "terrorist" and "Communist" as he's been fed to us. And I stare at him. He looks so frail from all the years of hardship. His voice is slightly reedy, but he talks without hatred. His eyes are screwed up and weak, but they are soft and engaging.

Something in my heart finds peace that day.

"This is the beginning of the end," says Paul bitterly.

But the other one, Terre'Blanche, is another story. He can talk like a preacher. The fact that he can address a crowd of our people doesn't come as a surprise. It isn't how he says it, but what he says. His words are laden with murder and mayhem.

"He's just the mirror image of the ANC's armed forces, Mother," Paul steps into the breach. "We are not going to be slaughtered like the Jews of old without a fight."

"I thought he had it in for the Communists?" I ask in response to a discussion on the radio where they explain the three sevens of the Afrikaner Weerstands Beweging *(Afrikaner Resistance Movement)* emblem in opposition to the 666 of the antichrist.

"Yes," Paul says almost dramatically, "and now De Klerk let the ANC and the Communists loose amongst us. With the fall of the Berlin Wall everybody thought it was the end of them. Looks like the news hasn't reached the ears of this lot yet. That's why Terre'Blanche saddles up his horse," Paul lamely justifies it.

"And poor De Klerk with all his good intentions is stuck in the middle and has to put out fires on both sides. As soon as the one tries to build up our image out there, the other quickly breaks it down," I reason.

Three voices are calling us out of the wilderness and all three voices are equally compelling. It depends on what you want to hear.

It is already dark when a bewildered Amos arrives out of the blue.

Ester is trying to sort out the bird's nest on Tossie's head and the tears are flowing. You would have thought that she would have worked it out after four and a half years. But no. The unfamiliar remains unfamiliar. The lessons she had learnt from her own curls didn't count here.

I can still hear the screams of my own children ringing in my ears to this day.

It's a task she takes on with a heavy heart, because it was never her intention to hurt the child.

It's funny, you would've thought their hair was as course as steelwool, when Ester told me to feel for myself one day. His hair was squeaky clean and as soft as a fleecy cloud. Just shows you how your eyes can deceive you.

Once Amos has reassured us that it's not about Emily, there is immediate relief. It was clear that Sterk-fontein wouldn't release her just like that. If ever.

The church is basically finished and plans are already afoot for the inauguration. The pews and the pulpit were carried in last week. It was a big moment for Paul.

As people are wont to do, Amos tries to keep his side of the story as simple as possible.

He apparently arrived at the church grounds in the late afternoon and discovered that all his belongings were gone. It transpired that certain members of the APK kicked the door down and threw all his things over the fence into the street. Some of the passersby and builders thought it was Christmas and his things were taken as quickly as our country was, until there was nothing left.

"What possessed them," Paul asks with quiet belligerence.

Amos, almost unconsciously, takes the wide-toothed comb out of Ester's hand and plumps up the child's frizzy hair. Without explaining, he shows her how to push the comb against the scalp and gently release the hair until it is standing dead-straight. And the child becomes as still as a mouse. A good thing too, or you would never have heard the story above the screaming.

"I don't know, my Master. They say we were making a noise," he says as if butter wouldn't melt in his mouth, and gives the comb back to Ester.

"It's a scandal," says Ester as she busies herself.

Paul has his own suspicions, but he learnt as a journalist that a story always has two sides. Paul storms into the entrance hall in a fury where the phone is plugged in.

There are good evenings made: "It's Paul here," followed by questions about what happened.

Firstly there is a long silence on this side as Bertie explains on the other side. He is given ample chance to put his case forward and Paul listens patiently. Now that the child is calm and settled, you can almost hear word for word how Paul snaps at Bertie when he gets the chance.

"Why didn't you at least call me if there was a problem," he begins calmly. "Yes, yes, I know how irritating a radio can be at that time of night, but you don't understand ... But of course I feel responsible ... I was the one who suggested that he go and stay there in the first place ... It doesn't matter! I've known the man for many years. He lived at our house ... And when there was a problem we discussed it and resolved it like civilised human beings!" he almost shouts and slams the phone down in the man's ear.

"I told you so," is written all over Ester's face when he walks back into the lounge.

He has a notebook and a pen in his hand.

"And?" is all she asks.

As we already know him by now, he looks as if he

has an article or a letter in mind.

"Amos, what exactly did they throw out?" he asks as if conducting an interview.

"Everything. I'm sorry, my Master."

"Your blankets?"

"Yes."

"They were brand new. We bought them not even three months ago," Ester reminds him.

And Paul writes.

"And your clothes?"

"Yes, my pants. Two shirts. No it was three, and a pair of shoes. Luckily I was wearing these. It was an old pair. My new jersey. And they broke the cups and plates and things that you gave me."

"Ah, it's a disgrace," I add.

Paul shows Ester what he is writing.

"I think it could be even more. I'm not too worried about the cups and plates."

Paul takes his time and he writes.

He looks up deep in thought and ponders for a while. As an afterthought he scribbles something in the notepad.

The next time he opens his mouth, he renders me speechless.

"Let's sue them."

"The Church? You mean the ..." is all that I get out.

"For Five Hundred Rand. For damages. And for theft!"

And standing in front of me is the Paul I know so well. What's right is right. What's wrong is also wrong. I've learnt to expect nothing less from him.

He will never cease to amaze me.

We've reached the end of the first year of the nineties and the case will have to wait until the beginning of the New Year.

Paul's angel wasn't without blame. It comes to light that there had been carousing and noise on the church grounds that had to be seen to be believed.

Ester is busy arranging roses early in the morning when I ask her directly. Her roses this year are beautiful, despite little rain and the late-year heat. She believes, the earlier you cut them in the morning, the longer they last. And with a bit of Jik and a spoonful of sugar in the water, Ester's artwork can last for up to two weeks.

"Oh. Ma, it's as if Paul wants to protect Amos against the whole world."

She sticks another stem in and stands back to inspect her handiwork.

"He came from the Transkei and didn't know much about what goes on here. He grew up in a homeland. He was a boy when he came to seek his fortune in the city."

She takes the last rose out of the vase again and trims it a bit.

"Just think, Ma. Just think what a shock it must have been for him when he walked into a post office for instance for the first time and there were separate entrances. Dammit," she swears in front of me. She quickly sucks her finger where the rose thorn pricked her.

"There was nothing like that where he came from."

She stands back satisfied, clearing away the leaves and cuttings.

"He probably knew about it, but had never experienced it before. I think this is the reason that Paul is doing what he's doing."

But between the incident and the court case much water flows under the bridge, in a manner of speaking.

In the same way that Ester never got involved in serving tea at church, she stayed away from political meetings and the likes.

How Paul talked her into it is beyond me, but they leave here for Pretoria on the sixteenth of December. I think she simply wants to reward him for what he did for Amos.

When they get to the Monument the smell of pancakes and boerewors (*sausage*) is everywhere. Everywhere there is *braai*-ing and people getting together.

There are far too many young people in Khaki for her liking. She can overlook the older generation, but it is the little ones who don't have an understanding of these things that worry her. And on every second sleeve there is that strange sign which resembles Hitler's emblem.

Paul crosses to one of the stalls to get something to eat.

"Ester, what do you want?"

"Nothing," she says spiritlessly. "I just lost my appetite."

Something happens on the stage which catches Ester's attention. Hanging on the one side is a huge banner which reads: *"Change back to the Trinity of God."*

The Master of Ceremonies tries to attract the attention of the crowds.

"Ladies and Gentlemen. Ladies and Gentlemen, can we have silence for a minute, please!" he tries in vain.

Most people ignore him. A few stop momentarily, but quickly carry on with what they are doing.

Paul arrives back with a boerewors roll in one hand and a pancake in the other for dessert.

Ester stands like Lot's wife of old, shaking her head non-stop as if she's got the shakes of the elderly.

Meanwhile a woman walks onto stage and starts singing. She sings the *Our Father*.

Paul piously stops eating.

There are people milling around everywhere handing out pamphlets. A young boy shoves one into Ester's hand. Without looking she dumps it in her handbag.

Reverend Shaw does the Reading in English of all things. To Paul it is a milestone, but he rather says nothing. He can see that Ester is lost in her own world.

The Reverend reads from the Lamentations of Jeremiah 1:3:

"Judah's people are helpless slaves, forced away from home. They live in other lands, with no place to call their own – surrounded by enemies with no way to escape. No-one comes to the temple now to worship on the holy days. The girls who sang there suffer, and the priests can only groan. Her city gates stand empty and Zion is in agony. Her enemies succeeded; they hold her in their power."

Then Paul's reason for coming walks onto the stage. For the first time Ester sees the man, from the poster that Paul had hung above Tossie's bed, in real life. He conducts the sermon well, faithful to his first calling, before politics swallowed him up.

The only thing that Ester has ever asked about this man is why he, as the KP leader, has never crossed the floor to the APK? He is and remains NG. Paul never has an answer for her.

Now she stands, looking in astonishment at the man, but her thoughts are somewhere else. Near the end she surfaces again and hears his overbearing closing.

"And that we, as representatives of our nation, will here bow before God as true believers in His Word; will worship and praise Him; and that the crowds here today in humility will undertake, before God and each other, to be a nation for God!"

Ester turns around and heads for the hills. Something has upset her. She moves like a bat out of hell. Paul tries to catch up with her. She's on her way to the parking lot. He never manages. She's got the head start of twenty two years in her stride. He eventually gets to the car gasping for breath where she stands impatiently yanking at the door handle. She wants to get in at all costs.

"What's wrong now," he puffs and pants.

"I want to get out of here ..."

"Why?"

"Right now!" she threatens him.

Paul quickly unlocks the door for her, because he can see that she's ready to tear him limb from limb today.

She climbs in. She slams the door just that bit too hard.

Once Paul has sat down, she looks him straight in the eye. And she looks. And she keeps on looking. She is white around the mouth. When she eventually opens her mouth she emits a sound like a knife. Not sharp. Not loud. Cutting.

"That was the first and the last time! I will not be a part of this."

And Paul knew then that he would never be able to ask her again.

The child and I are alone all day and it is like the old days with my grandchildren. He is angelic. When he isn't watching TV, he is playing with his cars in and around my feet.

I hear the door slam when they get home. She greets me and disappears into their bedroom. Paul goes to the kitchen and reappears with a cup of coffee in each hand. He just shrugs his shoulders. He puts one down for me and disappears down the passage with the other. I hear his "Ester, Ester" from the end of the passage and he arrives back cup in hand.

When he comes to sit down I feel sorry for him. Tonight he looks old. He almost seems to shrink next to me.

Ester emerges out of the bedroom with red swollen eyes.

As always I am busy with my crotchet-work and am wearing my glasses. The light in the lounge is brighter than the previous place and a side-lamp isn't necessary.

In her hand is a pamphlet. She holds it out for me to read. It is in large print and there are few words.

"Ma, and I heard someone there say: 'If it's not Terre'Blanche, then this is the thing that's going to save us.'"

And I read:

"*Stop open hospitals. Blacks are the carriers of AIDS. They are also carriers of lice. One bite and you're contaminated.*"

"And then they sang the *Our Father*," and she looks in Paul's direction and she repeats, "The *Our Father*, Ma. As if they deserve forgiveness. The world has been right all along!" Her voice almost becomes a whisper when she asks: "What kinds of sub-humans have we become, Ma?"

And Ester throws the pamphlet down at Pauls' feet.

This is another dark cloud that is beginning to descend on our country. In '82 we heard about this thing for the first time.

"This thing is not going to weigh on my conscience, Mother. It's the fault of the Oppenheimers and their single quarters. They brought the men in to dig for gold and ever since then they've been bed-hopping."

"But, Paul, the homelands are one and the same thing. The men have to survive without their women for months."

"It's not just about that. There are daily warnings, but they fall on deaf ears. When I talked to Amos about it, and told him that we don't want another baby here, and that he must use a condom, he said dismissively: 'No, Master Paul. That thing kills babies. If we kill them, who's going to look after us in our old age?' And others think it's a plot by the whites to control their numbers. We only have one life to live. Now it's every man for himself. If they don't want to learn, they must feel the sting themselves."

The newspapers and the news predicted this week that, at the turn of the century, a minimum of one million people amongst us would have died from this thing.

"Ma, if so many adults die, do you realise how many babies will be left behind?" is Ester's concern. "Where are we going to get the hands to help bring them up? When the Germans looked for homes for their orphans after the war, many of our people opened their doors wide. Look at Paul and his first wife, Ma. We'll just have to wait and see."

Amos's case comes up in the second week of the new year. Paul's decision to take on the APK, is in Amos' favour. He leaves the court that day with the prospect of Five Hundred Rand in his pocket.

But the after effect that this case will have on Ester and the family, no money can put right. It is mid-week and I am at Baby's place as per usual, when she walks through the door and vehemently throws *Die Transvaler* down on the bed next to me.

"Look at how he drags our family name through the mud with his big mouth, and this for a kaffir!" Baby barks.

At this stage we weren't so sure what you were or weren't allowed to call a black, but everyone knew that this was unacceptable. Even the word *'boer'* had in the meanwhile become a swearword.

"What are you supposed to call someone who lives and works on a farm, then, if you can't call him a *'boer'*?" I asked innocently one day.

"Probably a thing of the past!" is Ester's joke.

"Policeman is called Saddam and a kaffir," was the heading in *Die Transvaler*.

Police are investigating a charge of crimen injuria against Mister Paul de Villiers, a town councillor from Roodepoort, after he allegedly swore at a black court official at the Roodepoort Magistrates Court.

The seventy-five year old Mister De Villiers, a retired agricultural editor from an English newspaper, confirmed yesterday that he was involved in a language incident at the courts. He got annoyed when a court official wouldn't speak Afrikaans to him and allegedly called him a "f... dog". Mister De Villiers had taken his gardener to court to witness in a case of robbery. The man's six-year old son, Tossie, whom Mister De Villiers and his wife have brought up as their own, was with him."

Paul, Amos and Tossie leave early that day to appear in court on time.

With Ester at work, there is no other solution but to take Tossie along. Ester laid his church-clothes out early so that he could at least look his best.

Paul should have known better.

Tossie has the laws of Leviticus laid down the whole way there – about keeping quiet and sitting still.

"It's like church, but worse," Paul explains. "You mustn't move a muscle."

Amos goes into the court room and Paul and Tossie sit in the gallery. Paul half-waves at Amos, when he looks around, to make sure he knows where they are sitting. He waves back. His waving attracts the attention of the representatives of the APK, as well as Bertie, and they are whispering behind their hands amongst themselves.

The next minute there is a hubbub in the gallery when the court official orders Paul and Tossie out of court.

It is the Magistrate's sharp stare and his "Silence in Court" that sends Paul apologetically out the door.

Down in the court Willie Kotze, a court reporter, grabs his bag and notebook and leaves the court room.

"What do you mean ... I can't take the child into court?" Paul becomes hostile towards the court official who is now standing and ordering him around.

"I'm sorry, I do not speak Afrikaans," responds the court official.

Paul ignores his plea and asks in Afrikaans: "What am I supposed to do with the child? Was I supposed to leave him to his own devices?"

"Could you please repeat that in English?" the man repeats his request.

This triggers Paul's temper.

"Don't come tell me that you don't speak Afrikaans.

You know just as well as I do that it was compulsory at school," he reminds him and asks: "What's your name?"

"You can't force me to speak Afrikaans and you don't need to know my name," he replies dismissively.

"Go and find someone who can," orders Paul and rechristens him there and then: "Saddam Hussein!" It pours out of his mouth without a thought and the court official's back straightens like a poker.

"You called me what?" he bites back.

And Paul flings "Saddam" at him again.

The news headlines these days are crammed full of stories of Saddam Hussein and his murders of his own people. The leading story in this very newspaper claims that *"Saddam Hussein is a clever genius."*

Paul's commentary a week or so ago was in fact that it's good that these stories, mostly for the sake of the blacks, must be spread far and wide so that they can thank their lucky stars for the treatment that they get in this country.

"The world should get involved over there, instead of here, and do something about that." Paul said glumly. "What we've got here works. And has worked well for fifty years. That is, until they started interfering. They must rather go and boycott there. But no! If they do it in Iraq then Saddam will close the oil wells and then all the finger-waggers will feel the pinch. People are liberal until it starts costing them."

"You still can't take the child into the court room," the court official arrogantly replies because, after all, Paul is breaking the rules on his turf and the man knows the rules. And adds: "It's the father's problem, not yours."

In one slick move Paul sweeps the child up and onto his hip and look the man directly in the eyes.

"I am the child's father!"

With that he turns around and makes for the exit. He doesn't get far because the court official's words in perfect Afrikaans stop him dead in his tracks.

"You fucken dog!" he snarls at Paul.

I knew about the f... word, but had never heard it with my own ears, at least not used against someone. All I know is that it is the lowest of the low.

Paul slowly turns around. He gently puts the child down. He marches up to the court official and jabs his finger under the man's nose.

"Kaffir, I'll beat you up!" He says putting the man in his place.

He picks Tossie up and walks away. After a few steps he turns back. The man takes a few steps back because he doesn't know what's coming and Paul is a big man.

"And if you want to report me to the police for calling you that, then there is something that you need to know," Paul hits back at him in English. "My name is Paulus Daniël de Villiers."

Paul is unaware of the onlooker with the flapping ears who has listened in on the whole conversation.

Calmly he and Tossie walk out the door.

And there he is on the front page of a number of newspapers and with the titanic K-word. And we are dying of embarrassment.

Name-calling is not nice. And going too far is going too far. No matter what they say.

They refer to people like me as "lumps of lard." And it made me mad. Stark raving mad. On one or more occasion. That's when I thought: Good Heavens, I am a lump of lard. From their point of view. But it still never feels good to hear it.

Until one day I am standing in front of the mirror. And looking back at me is a lump of lard. And I start laughing. It doesn't suddenly make it any better. But I don't care anymore. And the name no longer holds any weight. You can never laugh it away. Because there are words and then there are words!

But the story didn't just land in the newspaper, Ester tells me. Paul was caught red-handed by this snake in the grass of a journalist.

It is late afternoon and Ester and Amos are busy in the garden.

Tossie is kicking a plastic ball that Paul recently bought for him, up and down the driveway. I see how in his element he is when he sees his own people playing soccer on TV. The child soon became adept at kicking because, like Ester, he was quick to learn. The next minute the ball flies a hair's breadth past her head and she ducks.

"Be careful. Next thing you'll break another window again, my child," she comments evenly.

Ester is turning the soil with a garden fork, because, what with the gravel and the clay that sticks together, it's easier to dig with a fork than with a spade.

Amos is trying to get the new seedlings into the ground as quickly as possible.

At the time of the court case Paul and Ester had been keeping an eye on him, because they needed him to be sober on the day that he gave testimony.

A car stops in the driveway. Dawie Marais climbs

out.

"Can you believe it ..." she mumbles to herself when she recognises him.

Ester drives the fork deep into the clay, because gardening equipment is plain dangerous with an unthinking child around. She removes her rubber gloves. She wears the gloves, not because she's putting on airs and graces, but because she has been digging the soil for as long as she can remember.

It took us years to teach her to give up the pleasure of eating clods of soil. It's apparently an iron deficiency that makes children eat sand, I had heard on Dulcie van den Bergh's *Hospital Hour.*

On the plot the soil was like peat and easy to work with. The red soil here, which turns into slippery clay when watered, we remember well from our days on the farm. When it rains here I steer clear of it or I fall easily. Then I rather stick to the cement pathways.

It takes a lot of effort to get the red from under the nails when it's taken its hold there, hence the gloves.

She meets Dawie halfway. His camera bag is slung over his shoulder and he sees the question in her eyes.

"I'd rather not leave it in the car. Afternoon, Aunty Ester."

They kiss as is customary for the Afrikaner.

This kissing over and over again with arriving and leaving, especially on a Sunday, gets a bit much for me. It leaves me feeling spent. But kiss you will because then you are greeting properly.

She knows him from Paul's days as a journalist, hence the familiarity.

"I'm scared they'll steal my bread and butter," he

says referring to his camera bag.

"Paul's on the phone," she explains. "Go in so long." She wipes the sweat from her brow with her sleeve. "A person could die from heatstroke out here. Go take a seat and I'll make us a cup of tea in the meanwhile."

He aims for the front door. In the foyer he bumps into an irritable Paul.

"That's right," he hears Paul say. "That's correct, Captain Bester."

Paul sees him and covers the receiver.

"It's the police. They want me to confirm something that happened at the courts yesterday," he whispers. "Take a seat; I'll be with you soon."

Paul resumes his phone conversation.

"Are you telling me that if I call him a 'kaffir,' after he's called me a f… dog, that it is only my fault. What was I supposed to do? Should I have called him 'Sir' and thanked him for it?"

He shakes his head despondently.

"And I'm going to write a letter to the Commissioner of Police, because I want to know why there are so many policemen at the courts, when they would do more good in Soweto, with all the violence happening there."

He cuts the conversation short with a "goodbye" and walks to the lounge.

"And Amos," Ester gestures around the edge of the beds. "Here you plant the Pansies at the front and the Afrikaners behind. Then we won't be bugged by aphids this year."

"It's because they really stink," Amos gives his two cents worth about the Afrikaners (*the local name for Marigolds*).

Just after the first leaves appear, the Afrikaners are already in bloom, and the stench is exactly like the dreadful Kakiebos (*Tommy-weed*).

"It's all the same in love and war," Ester agrees and smiles knowingly.

She rinses her hands under the outside tap and walks around the house. She kicks off her gardening shoes at the back door and slips on her house shoes that she leaves waiting there. It's bad enough having the child and the dog's red footprints all over the house and as an adult she knows better.

By this time Paul and Dawie have shaken hands and they've got passed the "How are you?" "No, fine and you?" phase and Paul has settled himself on the couch. The next minute Tossie bursts through the front door and plonks himself on Paul's lap, as he always does.

"And who's this?" Dawie pretends to be surprised.

"He's like our own child," says Paul and stops Dawie in his tracks.

Paul had stopped making excuses for the child's presence and behaviour long ago.

"How long has this been going on?" Dawie fishes for information.

"It's been four and a half years since they had to take his mother away."

"And his father?"

"That's his father outside in the garden."

He feels relaxed with the man. After all they were colleagues.

Paul looks lovingly at Tossie and pulls him close against his chest.

"He's such a lovely child. And so bright. Bright as a

button for his age. He goes everywhere with us and then yesterday ..."

Paul is dejected.

"What happened?"

"They wouldn't allow him in court."

"Court is court ..." and Dawie shrugs his shoulders.

"I know. But what was I supposed to do?"

"Well, he's a child, and children aren't ..."

"In this neighbourhood he's welcome everywhere," he says as if thinking aloud.

Paul has the pride of a father and is slightly emotional. His voice becomes croaky. He gets up and excuses himself.

"I'm quickly going to see why Ester's taking so long with the tea. My throat is bone dry."

Dawie and the child are left alone.

"And what's your name?" he asks for the record.

"Tossie."

"Tossie?" Dawie repeats questioningly about the child's strange name.

"Tossie, my Sweetheart's little KP-*kaffertjie*," rolls off his tongue and Dawie's eyes nearly pop out of his head.

It's something that Paul, as with "Master" and "Miss," had jokingly imprinted in his brain. And the child knows no better. It is offensive to Ester.

At that moment Paul walks in, tray in hand.

"I see what you mean. He's got an answer for everything."

Dawie stands and takes a cup from the tray that Paul is patiently holding.

"And as handsome as they come."

Ester comes in with a milk tart that she'd baked that

---

morning.

"Aunty Ester, have you got photos of Tossie?"

Ester hands Dawie a side plate and a serviette and dishes him a piece of tart.

"Baby photos. Nothing recent."

"Why don't I take a photo of you two and Tossie, and I'll send it to you as a memento."

"Ma, when he made this suggestion, I could feel the hair on my neck standing up straight, and I put him in his place with an answer, which if he knows women, he would understand."

"I'm not photogenic. Call it vanity. Call it what you will. If Paul wants his photo taken ... it's his decision. I'm going ... um ... to make a fresh pot of tea," and she makes herself scarce.

"I told Paul that night that I trusted Dawie as far as I could throw him, but Paul was gullible. He and that Willie-character were partners in crime, and because Paul only knew Dawie as a photographer, he fell hook, line and sinker for his story," she tells me while shaking her head.

The next day, after the name-slinging article, it was raining newspapers again. Once again in *Die Transvaler*, there for all to see on page three were Paul and Tossie.

In different circumstances I would have thought it was a lovely photo, but with the accompanying story that moment was ruined for me forever.

"*KP-man and his little black shadow*" – Willie's article smacks me between the eyes.

"*I am Tossie, Sweetheart's little KP-kaffertjie,*" the little *six-year old black boy says and he settles himself comfortably on the lap of Mister Paul de Villiers, a Town Councillor of the Conservative Party in Roodepoort.*

Mister De Villiers and his wife, Ester, are childless and the smooth-talking and high-spirited Tossie compensates handsomely for that.

Mister and Missus De Villiers, in a sense of the word, adopted Tossie when his mother, who worked as a domestic for them, was admitted to a mental institution. Tossie's father sometimes works for them in the garden in exchange for the servant's quarters.

According to Mister De Villiers, Tossie is so attached to them after four years that he follows them around like a shadow, even when they go out on business.

During the day he makes himself at home in the house and helps himself to food and drinks.

Because Tossie is so conversational and makes friends easily, he is always the centre of attention. He comes out with the most priceless sayings.

In the region of Mister De Villiers's house in Willow Avenue, Roodekrans, Tossie is a popular playmate of many white children. He is welcome in many of their homes and some of the children's mothers give him clothes.

Tossie has learnt to speak a smattering of English in the neighbourhood park. Tossie goes to school next year, and the De Villiers' are considering sending him to school in the coloured area, Davidsonville.

Although Mister De Villiers is in strong opposition to the government's restructuring policy, open white schools now offer other options.

The English-speaking Primary School, Ridgevale Primary, is just around the corner from Mister De Villiers' house and if the school is open to all races by then, Tossie could start his school career there.

Missus De Villiers says that Tossie is addicted to television and can spend hours in front of the box. A lot of the knowledge he has under his belt he gets from television. He is very clever for his age.

Tossie got his name because he couldn't pronounce his nickname, Tsotsi.

The story about the school is a new tune that I haven't heard before. And it strikes a false chord somewhere in my head.

But the assertion that Paul has acted outside of the law is mentioned nowhere beats me. If the journalist had been looking for a stick to beat him with, then it would have been *The Group Areas Act*, the only one that was still being enforced, and one that Paul was fighting to keep intact.

"When the English were in power and before Hitler's war, the whole world thought our policy was good," Paul answers me with a History lesson. We are busy with the afternoon's dishes. He washes and I dry. "It was the only solution. Then they committed large scale genocide there in the North. In the so-called cradle of civilisation. White on white. For a long time everybody just stood and stared, and did nothing. Because for a moment it looked like a solution, I mean with the Jews. And since then, the whole world has been singing another tune. And they call us inhuman. Inhuman, my foot."

He rinses the dishes and patiently hands them to me one by one.

I remember the time. My husband sat for who knows how long in a Ceylon jail, making heirlooms by hand. He made six "riempie" chairs (*with a woven leather seat*); also two with armrests; and a bench which was long enough for you to lie flat on. That long. And for what? How did that war affect us in reality?

Now he starts scouring the pots and I watch him. I've never know a more handy man. And he does it thoroughly.

"The lesson we had to learn from that is that blonde isn't better. And three years later, we write it into the law book," I say cheekily.

"They still don't understand our problem," he protests and scours even harder. "We are sitting on the edge of extinction. We are a small handful up against the masses. We haven't stripped the land bare of indigenous people, like in America and Australia. Maybe then our situation would have been different today. And look at how they look down on us. It was already in the late twenties that some of the churches damned it as unchristian. That is, the killing off of our blacks, Mother. It was one of the three options. The other was to add the milk to the coffee and turn it brown. That was unthinkable. And the last was to separate the goats and the sheep. You know, Mother, the Belgians next to the French; and the Hollanders next to the Germans. They all look the same, but they don't speak each other's languages and they also don't share a culture. They are different people and they belong apart. We didn't build a wall like in Berlin. There the same people were separated through politics. And they want to talk! We now cordon the camps off so that each can look after themselves in their own way. Next to each other. Not amongst each other. Separated by borders."

By now he has finished washing and is waiting for the water to drain.

"All that Verwoerd wanted to do was to divide up

kind by kind and to send them back to where they came from."

For a moment I want to laugh. I see our Afrikaner race being posted in bits and pieces to Holland, Germany and France. Back to places and things we know nothing about. All that we know about Holland is Tulips and cheese and about the tower in Paris. The Germans eat pork and we know even less about the Belgians. It's only the sound of our language that reminds us of them. We don't know them.

When the last of the water and foam have disappeared down the drain, he wipes the sink with a dry cloth, so that not even a mark is visible.

"And where do you think Verwoerd came up with this plan, Mother? He went back to where he came from. He returned to Holland where he was born. There they got the recipe right. In Amsterdam, where Marieke comes from, they've thought this through. They are doing it there to this day with religion. They call them pillars. Pillars to hold the temple up."

And I wonder who the hairless, blind Samson is; and who the Delilah is who is going to stand and laugh as the roof caves in.

Now he paces back and forth packing away the dishes. By now he knows the inside of the cupboards as well as any woman.

"Here it has a colour," I remind him. "It is all that the world sees."

"You don't put black and white washing together. And that's what they want. But then you get grey. Mother, you would know better than I do. Here in the city with a black in every backyard, we are bound together like music notes. And everyone plays beautifully together. Each in his place. Over there they don't know any better. However over here that's how we live in harmony. But we don't know the masses. Those in the townships. The faceless ones."

"And where does Tossie fit into the picture?" is all that I want to know.

Without answering, he walks out of the room.

The article in the *Roodepoort Record* had a completely different slant: *"Know your councillor: Paul de Villiers."*

Mister Paulus Daniël de Villiers, resident of Roodepoort since 1941, is the representative of Ward Three on Roodepoort City Council.

Mister De Villiers, who is retired, obtained a first class matriculation pass with distinctions in Wolmaransstad, and later went to obtain his Bachelor of Arts degree, an Honours degree and a Master's degree.

Before his retirement Mister De Villiers had an interesting and varied working life which included journalism, as well as experience in various other fields including service with the Meat Board, the Johannesburg City Council and Sasol.

Mister De Villiers' Ward on the council is the area west of CR Swart Avenue, from the junction with Ontdekkers Road. His Ward stretches to Ruhama Avenue and continues along this road to the railway line. It continues along the railway line to the boundary of Krugersdorp.

A supporter of the Conservative Party, Mister De Villiers describes himself, in political terms, as a follower of the late General JBM Hertzog. Mister De Villiers says he did not belong to any political party during his years as journalist, so that he could remain impartial, but joined the Conservative Party on his retirement from journalism as this party reflected his conservative view of political events.

Mister De Villiers is married to Ester Wilhelmina and the couple has an adopted son and two grandsons from his first marriage.

He is a leading member of his congregation of the Afrikaanse Protestantse Kerk onder Blanke Afrikaners.

Mister De Villiers says that he has not represented the Roodepoort City Council on any committees or at any seminars since his election to council due to the National Party's policy of nominating only National Party councillors to represent the council.

This, he believes, effectively prevents Conservative Party councillors from serving the people of Roodepoort in wider capacities.

His ideals for his Ward include maintaining the Ward's existing First World character with his voters retaining their own facilities, without them being "forced out" by members of the "Third World."

He would like to see his ratepayers continue to have their own schools for their own children.

Much of the squatter problem, which existed in his Ward, has been resolved but he wanted the total prevention of settlement of squatters in his Ward.

Among the achievements in his Ward since his election Mister De Villiers mentioned improvements to streets and pavements.

This article goes to print before the hiatus and here he is still standing firm on *Apartheid* in schools.

"Ma," Baby says through clenched teeth. "Look at how he's straddling two worlds. Or does he suddenly think that Tossie's white? He wants to do the same as he does with

Church. Send him to the English, and the Afrikaans schools stay white. He's a hypocrite, Ma."

I silence her with "Love is blind." Also colour blind I keep to myself.

Funny, if you had to hear the child without seeing him, he's just another Afrikaans boy.

Nothing comes of going to church, because even at the service there is plenty of whispering through clenched teeth and flinging of accusations. And after the APK's defeat in court and all the articles, Ester and Paul lay low.

Absolutely nothing comes of the name-slinging. It is dismissed as "an eye for an eye," and the case is thrown out.

But now and again, day or night, when the phone rings, they are called Judas, Kafferboetie (*Kaffir lover*) and f... dog.

"We did nothing wrong. We did what we had to do for Amos. What's right is right, am I correct?" Paul tries to figure it out for himself.

"Try and explain it to them." Ester holds the receiver out to him. "And now, they've also got it in for the child."

"What is wrong with giving a child food? Clothing? Is it a sin?" He answers as a plea.

"They don't see it like that. They just see that he's black. They are here," is all she can muster.

He sees them coming through the window – the APK committee and the Minister.

And now Tossie also has to lie low.

"Tossie, you need to understand. We can't afford to make a mistake," Paul takes the child by the shoulders and looks him in the eye. "What do you do the minute a car stops at the gate or someone rings the doorbell?"

Tossie loves this game. He runs straight for the cupboard and disappears.

"That's good," Ester encourages him. "And Ma," she says as she rushes down the passage and pops her head in at my door. "Ma, keep an eye on him."

The doorbell rings.

"And in the future, if we're not here, please don't open the door, Ma."

I nod my head because this has been going on for the last week or so.

"Not even for family," Paul adds, also popping his head around the door. "The family, more than anyone, must not know that the child is still here."

And their heads disappear.

The front door opens and shuts and I know they are inside.

They go and sit in the lounge. Ester doesn't even attempt to be courteous and offer them something to drink.

"We know the child is still here," Ben Swart starts up at the front door.

Without responding immediately, Ester stares at him to see which way the wind is blowing.

"Mister Swart, can you see through the walls with those glasses of yours?" She is referring to the thick glasses which make his eyes look the size of saucers.

"No, but ..." he responds a bit gawkily.

"Because, if you can ..." she widens her eyes so that he can see she's joking, "you can look around with pleasure. To your heart's content. You'll see that only my mother is here. And us, of course."

Paul has a shorter fuse and comes straight to the point: "Say what you want to say."

"We, as elders of the APK," Dirk Mosterd begins with a very formal approach, "feel that you and your wife have undermined everything that we as a Church stand for."

And Ben plays his trump card: "You have overstepped ..."

"The most important law ..." Dirk quickly takes over.

"The only *Apartheid* law that still stands," Ben says with his saucer-like eyes and waits for a reaction.

Neither Ester nor Paul reacts.

"The one that us Conservatives are determined to uphold."

"We always thought that you were one of us," Ben hisses, narrowing his eyes.

"Don't preach to me about the law."

"Which law?" Ester asks naively.

The APK's glance furtively at one another. This isn't a conversation for a woman. It is a subject to be dealt with by men.

"*The Group Areas Act?*" she says, naming it for what it is.

"Oh, Missus De Villiers, women shouldn't worry their pretty little heads about politics," Dirk says with a grimace.

But Ester is on top form and won't be put in her place.

"Mister Mosterd, since I am not barefoot and pregnant in the kitchen, as you would like ..." she says in a measured tone.

"That's not what I meant ..." he says half apologetically, because he gets her meaning.

"It doesn't mean that I can't read, or think for myself." She taps her finger against her temple.

Paul's mouth literally hangs open. He can't believe what Ester is up to. And in front of the Minister.

Ben is annoyed, but keeps his cool. His wife would never in a million years dare to challenge him like this. And he looks at Paul, in the hope that he will silence her. Paul doesn't move a muscle.

"Seeing you understand everything so well, Missus De Villiers, you should understand that we can also have you prosecuted."

"Is that a threat?" Paul asks calmly.

Ester is not easily frightened.

"Or a promise of retaliation?"

After what seems like an eternity, Minister Fourie opens his mouth for the first time.

"Brother, Sister," he looks at Paul and then Ester, with his eyes settling on the other two. "The elders and deacons," he stresses, "they have decided, and insisted, that I withdraw your membership of the Church," he says sympathetically. "Aunty Ester, Uncle Paul, I'm so sorry."

"Thank you, Minister," she says softly. She accepts it in the spirit that it is intended.

Ester stands up deliberately. She points to the front door.

"Goodbye, Gentlemen." And she ushers them out.

Paul is dumbstruck. A staggering blow has been struck. The others leave. He remains seated.

"He, the Minister, won't last long," he says to me later and laughs 'til he cries. "And Ester," he wipes the tears from his eyes. "Ester can stand her ground against any man, Mother," and he doubles up.

But from laughter comes tears.

That evening everyone eats as if chewing razor blades.

"I don't know why they're making such a fuss. The fact that Amos went to court about their behaviour never made the papers. And they were justifiably fined for their actions," is Paul's argument. "It's the KP who worry me. It's their name that's been dragged through the mud, and if I feel shame about anything, it's the embarrassing situation I've put them in. And what have they done?" He waits for someone to make a comment.

Ester and I eye one another and, as if with one voice, we answer his question.

"Absolutely nothing!"

"Exactly!" he agrees.

It is astonishing that there had never been a threat of expulsion from the KP, or an expectation that he would give up his seat. Paul's appreciation of his party grows daily.

"They can see that I am just plainly doing my Christian duty," he echoes Ester's words from years ago.

I want to open my mouth about exactly this, but I know it's late and I'm not in the mood for an argument.

When I finish my business in the bathroom later than usual, through the open door I see Ester standing at Tossie's little bed. She's already in her gown, but I know sleep will evade her tonight. Her face is buried in her hands as if she can't bear to even look at the child. He's sleeping peacefully. She sighs deeply.

Tonight she looks her age. The worry has gouged deep lines around her eyes and around her mouth.

She pulls the blankets up around his chin. She softly strokes his tight curls.

I can no longer walk lightly and she knows I am

there.

"What are you going to do, my child?" I whisper as she walks to the door.

"To tell you the truth ..." and she looks back into the room in the hope that the answer is waiting there. "I don't know, Ma." She turns off the light and leaves the door slightly ajar. "All that I really know is that we're in hot water, and we need to get out of it."

The redness around her eyes makes her eyes even bluer.

Now it's time for me to give advice and comfort. I must be a mother to my child.

"He'll have to go."

It's not what she wants to hear. But it's the only solution.

Her "Oh, Ma" comes from a place deep inside where her sigh came from, cut open and raw.

"To his Ouma. And his sister," and her head finds solace on my chest. "In the meanwhile, until you find a solution."

Her head jerks against my chest. I understand the pain of saying goodbye to a child.

"I know ..." and I feel her tears soaking through my night dress right down to my heart. "At a crossroads there is always more than one direction that you can go in. I know you'll choose the right path."

"I hope so, Ma," she says in a tiny voice. "Let me help you to bed. It's late."

In the silence of my room I grapple with the almightiness of our Creator. The situations that we stumble upon are part of our lesson here on earth. When Paul chose the path out of the NG Church, where love of one's neighbour lost its colour, and hardened his heart against the second Commandment, God stepped in and began working to soften him.

"I don't know how we're going to find them," I hear Paul say outside my door on Sunday. "I called the number, but it's the number of the telephone booth in Chrissies-meer."

Since Mary's sudden departure, they had only got news from those quarters once or twice.

"When they're this small, they forget quickly. It's better this way. It's adults who hold onto things," he replies when I asked news of the little one. "You don't rub salt in your own wounds."

But the doll for her second birthday had been gathering dust in his wardrobe for years now. He could never let go of that.

"Then you must keep phoning until you get hold of them," Ester replies practically.

For the next two days there is praying and weighing up of all the possibilities and then mulling them over again and again.

There is only one solution.

It's early on Wednesday and there is much movement in the house. Ester put in leave for the whole week to think it through and eventually packed Tossie's suitcase and put some of his toys in a box.

"Ester," Paul says, looking into her eyes. "I know you're overwrought ... but please ... you must try not to cry in front of the child. He's already doesn't feel good about this."

"I won't cry."

Ester had somewhere in the depth of the night against all odds given over to this. By sunrise she was empty.

Paul phones and phones without any luck.

"Then we must go and look for them. From door-to-door if needs be," and she goes into Tossie's room. She puts on a brave face.

Tossie is sitting on the bed trying to tie his shoe laces. Ester throws the last of the clothes into the half-empty open suitcase and closes it. She kneels next to Tossie.

"Let me help you." There is a "for the last time" in her voice, but not in her words. "This one goes over, and the other one?" She looks up and sees no interest in this rhyme, "under and then we have a ...?" He doesn't respond again. "A knot. Now we make a ...? A bow." Like I had done with the nappy all that time ago, she lets the laces go without tying them. "Now it's your turn."

"I can't, Ma."

"There's no such thing as can't. Who do you think is going to do it for you when I'm not there?"

She cups his face in both hands and squeezes him softly so that his thick lips pout.

"It doesn't matter."

She quickly busies herself with the laces, stands him up and pulls his socks up over his knees, and folds them over twice. He's never fitted into clothes of his own age. Always a number or three smaller. He'd long remained a baby to Ester.

"Ma, I don't want to go," he says for the umpteenth time today.

Ester's heart stops.

"Why not? It's going to be great. You'll see," she

says, pretending to be excited, and smiles through her thickly swollen eyes. She almost sounds convincing. "You'll see Mary. Do you still remember her? And your Ouma and all your cousins? It's only for a little while. Think of it as a holiday. Once you're in school, you'll learn to appreciate holidays."

He doesn't fall for it. He's not used to being lied to and easily sees through her.

"I don't want to go."

Ester picks up the case. She puts out her hand for him to take it.

"Come."

He takes the hand that he knows and trusts and allows her to lead him out of the room.

They drive up the hill. They take a left into Ontdekkers. A hundred metres or so later they look right and in silence remember the good old days on the plot.

It's an endless road to Chrissiesmeer. It's approximately three-hundred kilometres from here. To get there, you drive in the general direction of Middelburg in the Transvaal and change direction towards Hendrina. The landscape's appearance changes before your very eyes into the beauty that the Highveld is well known for. Only at Breyten do the directions to their final destination start appearing.

The white, rose and dark-pink of the Cosmos at the roadside keep Ester mesmerized. They fly by and she gets lost in their simplicity.

They were brought here from overseas and yet they don't transplant easily. Their seeds need rest to germinate. If you turn the soil, you can forget about them. They flourish in places where there is no man or beast, all along the road. It's a hardy rogue which sees chance for grass and bushes, but little else. But I do wonder, if you were to take the seeds and really get to know their nature, surely it should be possible to plant them where you will. Create the correct conditions, and surely they will grow.

The silence of Ester and Paul's thoughts are suddenly interrupted from the backseat of the car.

"Sweetheart, Sweetheart, you need to stop. I want to wee," he pleads urgently.

Ester half-turns around and chastises him: "I told you to go before we left."

They had already stopped in Breyten to make sure of their directions and everyone had done their business.

"I did," Tossie reminds her. "I need to go again," and he crosses his legs to avoid an accident.

Paul watches him in the rear-view-mirror.

"You'll have to hold it in until we find a tree," he says when he catches Tossie's eye.

The Mazda slams on brakes and stops under a tree next to the sign that reads: *"Chrissiesmeer 25kms."*

The door opens and Tossie jumps out.

"Stay at the side of the road. Don't try to cross," Ester calls over her shoulder.

The minute his feet reach the ground he starts running so that all you can see is dust flying. He must have realized that this isn't any ordinary journey and took a chance for old time's sake.

Ester realizes what's going on, flies out the door, kicks off her high-heels, sending them flying, and goes after him in her stockings.

Passers-by must have found this a very strange sight.

A white woman chasing a black child can only mean one thing: He must have stolen something and she wants it back!

The tears dig furrows into her cheeks, in spite of her promise to Paul. After fifty paces Tossie is exhausted and sinks to his knees. His whole body heaves from the heartache. Ester goes down on her haunches next to him and puts her arms around him. And they stay like this until neither of them has any tears left to cry. When they have finished, they get up and walk to the car. Ester helps him into the car and goes in search of her shoes. Her stockings are in tatters and her left foot is covered in blood from the one stone that she misjudged. Stubbing a toe can be a sore thing, but it's the last thing on her mind. Ester gets into the back with him. And they continue the journey with Tossie curled up on her lap.

She is staring out of the window again, but this time she is counting down each kilometre, like the lime-stoned cement poles do, every one hundred metres nearer to the end. The end of an era when she was happy. And a time when she understood what it felt like to be fulfilled.

They resemble small white tombstones all along the road.

A kilometre before the town she reads: "Welcome to Chrissiesmeer," and her heart misses a beat.

The town partly has the big lake next to it to thank for its name – one of hundreds in the area – which also happens to be the largest inland lake in our country. The town is named after Christina, the daughter of Pretorius, an ex-president of the Transvaal.

This settlement is also well-know for the battle that

took place here at the turn of the twentieth century. Today it sports beautiful sandstone buildings, the graveyard and the ancient Oak trees that remind one of days gone by when we were at war with the English.

They stop a few times and ask about Tossie's family. Near the telephone booth Paul remembers that Evelina had said something about a Master Albert that she worked for. The only Albert is an Opperman, according to the shop owner.

They stop at the house. Paul gets out. Even before he reaches the front door, Albert is on his way out to meet him. Albert gestures in the direction of the township just outside the town. They say goodbye. The Mazda pulls away.

They drive into the township and turn right into the third street.

A little girl is playing outside in the dust. When she sees the car she runs screaming into the house. Evelina appears at the door.

Ester and Paul get out of the car.

Tossie peers through the window but doesn't move.

Paul sees the little girl who at first appears shyly in the doorway and then disappears behind Evelina. She clings to her Ouma's skirt and appears and disappears every time Paul looks at her. He turns around and from the boot fetches the doll that he had bought for her all that time ago. He kneels down next to her. He holds the present out for her to take it. She ducks out of sight behind her Ouma.

"Hello, Mary," he attempts quietly.

She doesn't know him anymore. To him she is prettier than ever. Mary turns around and runs into the house without taking the present. He gives it to Evelina. Sadly he turns around and goes back to the car. He is on the verge of tears.

"Evelina, he will have to stay here. It is maybe only for a little while," Ester says, keeping her emotions in check.

"But Miss can see that we are already so many."

For the first time she realizes that there are swarms of people standing around.

"If it's about money ... we will sort it out. If he needs anything, ask Master Albert. We will arrange things with him."

Ester walks to the car and opens the door.

"Come," and she puts out her hand. "Come and meet your family." Tossie gets out very subdued.

In the meanwhile Mary appears shyly at the door of the house. Ester notices.

"This is Mary. Your sister. Do you remember her?"

Tossie shakes his head.

By now Paul has unpacked everything. Evelina tells two teenage boys to help him. Unwillingly they carry Tossie's previous life into the house. Evelina holds out her hand. Tossie refuses to take it and instead hides behind Paul.

"He's not used to so many bl... so many people," Ester quickly corrects herself. "You'll have to be patient with him."

Ester kneels next to Tossie. She strokes his face. This dejected image is burnt into her memory.

"Don't worry. We'll see you soon," she attempts to put him at ease.

She takes his hand and leads him to Evelina. She places his hand in that of his Ouma.

"Let's go," she says resolutely.

Without saying goodbye she turns around and gets into the car. She's upset but her face is a blank palette.

Paul says a last little something to Evelina and gets into the car. He starts the car, opens his window, and waves. Tossie waves back.

Ester stares straight ahead.

The car pulls away in a cloud of dust. Only when they have gone a bit further does Ester dare to look back. The dust has settled and Tossie is still waving. The rest of them have gone inside.

Once again they stop at the Opperman's house. Albert's wife is sickly so they didn't get the chance to meet her. He looks like a good man. He's round about Paul's age.

Ester remains in the car. She is afraid her legs will let her down. She stares at her feet and for a brief moment she is ashamed of her stockings. For the first time she is aware of her big toe bleeding. The pain throbs like the ache in her heart.

Paul knocks on the window and she winds it down. She says "Hello" to the stranger that they are entrusting Tossie's welfare to.

"Ester, pass me Tossie's bank book."

Since his fourth birthday they have been putting a few Rand a month away for him. The rainy day that they had supposedly been saving for was upon them sooner than they could have imagined. Ester opens her handbag and gives it to him. Paul in his turn hands it to Albert.

"When it runs dry ... call us," Paul says as he writes their number on the back of the book.

Paul says goodbye, gets in and they drive off.

They pass a church. Suddenly Paul slams on brakes and reverses. Paul gets out and knocks on the door of the manse next door. He exchanges a few words with the man, gets back in the car and they leave.

"What's going to happen to him, Paul?" is all that Ester can ask.

She recognises the meagreness of his new home for what it is.

The corrugated iron sheets on the roof are held down with stones to stop the wind and here and there is an unbroken pane in a window frame. There is no sign of a cable for electricity or a pipe that suggests that there is water.

What you don't know doesn't hurt you; people are quick to tell you.

It was only when we arrived in the city with all its amenities that we wondered for the first time how we had done without them. If the power is off for even a day, and everything that you are used to stops working, you quickly remember the heat of a heater, a cooldrink straight out of the fridge, a light that switches on at the wall, a hot bath and a square box where your world unfolds before your very eyes. Without even mentioning a soft bed and three meals a day on the table.

"She didn't even know who I was," is Paul's disappointment.

When the article appears in the Sunday publication of *The Star*, Paul is furious.

"What has happened to journalism; the whole thing is full of mistakes! They no longer have respect for people's names. *'Tsotsi,'* I beg you."

And there he and the little one are seated again. Exactly the same photo.

"Black son comes second to KP," reads Leonard

Charleston's article.

He had made a few calls before knocking at Paul's door. With all the goings on at the church Paul had been quick to find Amos another job, because going back would have been impossible. The journalist must have tracked Amos down along the way somewhere, who knows where, because no-one had seen him for dust in the past week.

Mister Paul de Villiers has chosen the Conservative Party ahead of his "black son," and has found a new home for him in an Eastern Transvaal black area.

Controversy is still surrounding little Tsotsi Xele (5), after his father Amos had said that the boy was still living in the childless De Villiers house in the plush Roodekrans suburb.

However, when the Sunday Star visited the house yesterday there was no sign of the boy whom Mister De Villiers and his wife, Ester, described as a "very likeable and entertaining boy."

Mister De Villiers was visibly moved when he said how much they missed little Tsotsi. "Our house is empty without him," he said, "but he has to get schooling and he could not continue staying with us."

"It is sad that it has happened, but we realised that it would be an embarrassment to the Conservative Party," he said.

The boy now lives with his grandmother where, Mister De Villiers says, there is a good school as well as accommodation.

"We are sure that he will be well looked after," he said. "It is a nice school and is within walking distance from where he stays."

Mister De Villiers said he still had a "fatherly responsibility" towards the boy. "We shall see that Tsotsi gets whatever he needs and will pay for his education and accommoda-

tion."

The little boy was adopted four years ago by the De Villiers couple after his mother was admitted to a mental institution. He had been living in the household.

Mister De Villiers denies rumours that the boy would be put up for adoption. "That is certainly out," he said.

"Yes, we are missing him and will stay in touch with him," he said, "but we will give him time to settle in in his new environment. It is not easy. At first we will not go and visit him. It will just open wounds in our hearts."

"We asked a white family in the town where he stays now to keep an eye on him and to inform us if he needs anything," he said. "A relative of Tsotsi works for this white family. We will organise his finances through that family."

Mister De Villiers said they also asked the local white Mission Minister to visit him regularly.

He said he knew it was not easy for the boy, who left for his grandmother this week. "Still, he is just a kid and I do not think that it would have such a negative effect on him."

The 75-year-old Mister De Villiers said his colleagues in the Conservative Party were not angry with him.

"My problem is with the people of my church," said Mister De Villiers, a congregant in the local right-wing Afrikaans Protestantse Kerk. "Some of them gossip about it and I can't understand why."

Mister De Villiers said that even "critical" people could not help but love the cute little boy.

He said he did not find it strange that he as a member of the KP has a black child living in their house.

"Look, when his mother went to the mental institution we plainly saw it as our Christian duty to look after little Tsotsi."

Mister De Villiers said he had organised with Tsotsi's

father's new employers that they deduct a certain amount of his
salary to send to the little boy's new Eastern Transvaal home.

"We will however still support him," he said. "That
money will also go towards supporting his little sister who is also
staying with his grandmother."

Come the weekend and my visit, I can see how this
state of affairs has affected Ester. It has stolen her laughter
away.

With Tossie out of the house, this law that kept us
apart moved in and took its seat in the child's chair. He
wasn't a stranger to Paul. He was invited in and a place was
set for him.

"You don't choose with your heart, you choose with
your head. What's right is right. You can't get past that."

If Paul was as stupid as an ass, you could have
attempted to think up an excuse for him. You can lead a
donkey to water, but you can't make it drink. It needs to
happen on its own. And when I think that that donkey has
tried the water and has drunk of it, that's when I realize that
he has the kind of thirst that cannot be quenched.

"What we did was wrong, and now we're paying the
price," he says firmly. "That law was always our preservation and must remain in place," he defends himself.

It is in fact Paul and his self-righteousness that now
stands between him and me, because it is affecting my child.

Ester's silence becomes a scream in my ears.

She disappears into her workroom for hours on end
every day.

Aloneness covers her like a cloak. Because when she
looks around for support, there is nobody there.

For a while now my children and their children come visit me during the week. Many of them hadn't set a foot inside Paul's house for a long time. There are suddenly so many unexpected things happening by chance in their lives on a Sunday that I stop believing their excuses.

None of us understand what is going on anymore. Everybody has an idea, but is too afraid to ask.

"A person can talk to your heart's content, Paul, and you can approach it from all possible angles, but you cannot tell your own heart what to feel. Never mind have it prescribed to by a law. Look at the state Ester's in." I chastise him.

Milla's daughter, Annelien, pops in this week. Not to avoid Paul and Ester like the others, but more to come and talk about her concern for Ester.

There has always been a bond between them. Not like a mother and daughter and also not like between sisters. It just exists.

I had worked out that I had crocheted enough squares for a single bed. The border and the first row were in a kind of a royal blue and were a bit easier on the eye. The rest of the colours were predominantly shades of blue, green and, here and there, a bit of yellow to brighten up the blanket.

Annelien plonks herself down on the floor to help sort them out. You can't just put any pattern next to another or it ends up as an unsightly garish mess.

This is when she puts these ideas into my head. It is mostly my grandchildren, like her, who wish this thing away.

"Ouma," says Annelien, "it can't go on like this for

much longer. And I wish it was over. The world won't stop turning because a few people would like that."

She starts arranging the blanket on the carpet. My daughters were the last ones who could crochet. Annelien and her generation have studied and gone to work and will never do things like that. My own children have also broken away from the traditional family names.

"They have done away with all the other laws," and she looks up for a minute, "and what has actually changed for us? Nothing!" she says, shaking her head. "People are selective by nature," and she carries on sorting. "The fact that people can now intermarry is proof of that. It's not as if the whole world around us is filled with bastards as a result."

"You must sort them into a right-angle, in the exact proportions of the bed," I show her. "It's longer than it is wide. It's different to a double bed."

She adds an extra row on top and at the bottom. And there you have it.

"Ouma, you know how it's always been with our people," she continues. "If you arrive home with an Englishman, a Jew or a Catholic, there's a huge family drama. There are very few of us who would dare to arrive with someone of another colour."

"You're right," and I want to laugh. "Believe me; the blacks have the same problem. They don't marry easily outside their own kind."

"Exactly. But you can't dictate what the heart feels through a law book."

That's when I get what she's about.

"It's the same with the child. All that it's done is turn innocent people with feelings into criminals. That's all.

Ouma, we and our children are going to be held responsible for this thing one day. We didn't start it. It was there and we didn't know any better. We were brought up to believe that this is how it should be. At night the blacks disappeared somewhere so that we could play safely in the streets. And sleep safe and sound. In ignorance."

She stands up, steps back and surveys her handiwork.

"Because of this we never got to know them."

"What you don't know, the heart doesn't feel," we say almost together.

"But they know us inside and out, Ouma." She is suddenly very serious. "The sins of the fathers will be visited upon the children into the third and fourth generations. I think that's what Uncle Paul and the others believe. And that's why they're afraid. Afraid of what's still to come. That's why they're clinging to what they've got. Because people like them expect to be punished for this thing that we've done here."

In the coming days Paul spends more and more time with his Bible and on his knees. He is looking for answers. The answers that he wants to hear elude him.

But it is in the blessing and the prayers of thanks before and after meals that the other Paul's voice is heard. The Paul who stood up for Amos. The Paul who is father to Ester's little *Tsotsi*.

With the blessing he holds out his hand as always to take Ester's. When he asks that the hands that prepared the food be blessed, he always rubs Ester's hand softly in thanks for her efforts.

Her hand however now remains in her lap with her

Albert every week to find out how things are going with the child and to check on money matters. Albert says that, under the circumstances, things are going well. It is precisely the circumstances that concern Ester and she convinces Paul to go and see for themselves.

Albert says they came knocking regularly for odds and ends that Tossie apparently needed. It was when the requests became more and more outrageous that he tried to explain nicely to Evelina, that, yes, it's all good and well that the child might need washing powder and candles, but not cigarettes and hair straightener.

Once they have passed Albert and taken the gravel road, from far away Ester can see a group of children playing in the dirt outside the house.

Tossie sits apart from them. He doesn't join in.

The children scatter the minute the Mazda turns the corner. Ester hardly waits for the wheels of the car to stop turning and she's out of the car.

Evelina, who hears the car stopping, appears in the doorway.

Tossie gets up slowly, but doesn't come any closer. He just stands there. He looks battered. Ester sees that he sees her and opens her arms wide, expecting him to run into them like he did every afternoon when she came home from work.

"Hello, my child," she says with her heart beating in her throat.

He doesn't react.

He says nothing.

He simply stands there, staring at her with big eyes.

Paul walks over to where a dejected Ester is still on her haunches and helps her up.

"I think he's just a little shy. We last saw him four weeks ago," he attempts to reassure her.

Ester doesn't know him to be shy and she walks over to him. She kneels next to him. Carefully she takes his hand. His hand feels rough and dry in hers. His hair is caked with dust. His arms and legs are covered in sores.

Without greeting her, he pulls his hand away, and runs off, disappearing around the corner of the house.

Ester is bewildered.

"Ignore him ... and he'll come back of his own volition," is Paul's advice.

For the first time Paul becomes aware of the multitude of people swarming out of the house. His eyes search for one in particular. He recognizes Tossie's clothes on the bottom of every second child.

He notices Tossie peeping around the corner of the house.

Then the second head appears.

"Evelina, precisely how many of you are living here?" he wants to know.

"Sometimes twelve, sometimes fifteen."

He sees one of Tossie's cars lying in the dust and picks it up. The car looks as if it's collided with a truck – that's how flat it is.

"Master Albert tells us that the money is nearly finished," he says while examining the car from all sides. "That money was meant for Tossie and Mary. Not for everybody."

Tossie moves closer unnoticed.

"Look at what they look like!"

Mary is standing, half hidden, behind Tossie. Every now and then her head pops up shyly. As soon as Ester or

Paul makes eye contact with her, she disappears again.

Tossie, on the other hand, isn't joining in this new game. He just looks at them.

Paul tries another approach.

"Evelina, we'd like to take the children for a little drive."

"You two, get in the car," she orders them.

Mary quickly glances at Tossie. Only after an eternity does he respond.

Paul opens the back door and they get in very submissively.

They drive in silence to the town.

Ester leans over her seat and chats to the children on the back seat.

"Do you want cooldrink?" she asks. "Paul, pull over, we've just passed a café," and she whispers to him: "Look at what Tossie's arms look like."

People think that you can't see sunburn on black skin, and therefore not a bruise or a sore spot either. Ester knows every inch of this child and is familiar with each mark and blemish. She can see that something's wrong.

"I've seen," Paul says, almost moved to tears.

They drive around the block and stop outside the café.

When Paul gets out of the car, Ester tries again: "You've got a big family, Tossie ..."

The silence stretches between them. Both children are just staring at her. She tries again.

"You're going to school soon," she says trying to change the subject.

It's as if they don't hear her. Or don't want to hear her.

"Has the Mission Minister visited you yet?"

Just then Paul comes out of the café bringing relief. He's got a packet brimming with sweets and cooldrinks in his hand.

"Which one do you want, Tossie?" he asks as he gets in. When Tossie doesn't react, he tries Mary.

"Mary?"

She is just as quiet today as she was the last time. He realizes that she doesn't understand him. When she was taken away, she had just started to become understandable. The smattering of Afrikaans that she knew was limited even then. Paul holds the cooldrinks out one by one so that she can choose.

"I've got Coke, Raspberry, Creme Soda ..." and he turns quickly to Tossie. "I remembered how much you loved the green cooldrink."

Paul opens the cans and puts a straw in each. He first gives the green to Tossie and then the red to Mary. They take the tins and put the straws in their mouths without looking away for a second. Children do that. If they stare, they stare.

"Not a word. Not even a thank you," he mumbles as he turns back and starts the car.

Ester remembers the packet lying at her feet. She opens it and holds two Tinkies up in the air.

"Look at what I've got here. Your favourite."

He doesn't react.

Ester tears open the plastic wrappings and gives them each one. They take them without even a hint of enthusiasm.

"The rest are for later. Paul, let's go."

Once back with Evelina, Paul wants answers.

"Evelina, what's wrong with the children?" he asks intently. She just shrugs her shoulders.

"I don't know, my Master."

"We must go. Will you explain to them that we'll be back in two weeks time? It's far away."

He gives the children the packets with the rest of the treats and says goodbye.

"Goodbye, you two."

Neither of them responds.

"Ester, get in the car. Let's go."

Ester waves half-heartedly at the children.

Neither of them wave back.

They leave.

The silence of the children engulfs them and both get lost in separate worlds.

"It's when I'm in church ... that I miss him the most," Ester says with a lump in her throat, about twenty kilometres outside the town.

The car stops and turns back.

It is early evening when they get home.

While Ester runs Tossie a bath, supper is thrown together.

"Paul, hurry up. Come and look here!" she cries a bit later from the bathroom. Her voice is tinged with hysteria.

"What's wrong?" he calls from Tossie's room.

He is busy unpacking the child's belongings. The toys they just left strewn in the dust.

It's the urgency in her voice that causes him to hurry.

Tossie is in the bath. Ester is kneeling beside him. The bathwater is milky from the bath oil and the Dettol. It is when she starts sponging him down that she sees the extent of his condition. Children walk and fall from morning to night, but this is worse.

"Paul, look here."

Tossie's whole body is covered in sores and bruises.

"He's got lice," is all that Paul gets out. "What did you expect?"

"And the bruises, Paul?"

He just shakes his head.

"What happened, Tossie?" she asks without expecting an answer. It was the same story all the way from Chrissiesmeer.

Tossie doesn't respond.

"Talk to me." She grabs him by both shoulders and forces him to look at her.

"Why?"

If he doesn't respond now, she's going to shake him until she gets an answer. She stops herself forcibly.

His little voice is almost inaudible: "I don't know ..."

"Why?" she asks gently.

"It was when ... it was every time that I wanted to speak to them," he says with difficulty. A tear teeters on the ridge of his bottom lid.

"Who did it?"

The "who," "what" and "where" pour out of Ester's mouth. She wants clarity. But she isn't prepared for what she is about to hear.

"What did they do, my child?" she asks comfortingly.

"They hit me."

"And your back?" she asks and bends him over so that Paul can see his little back. The marks are in stark contrast to his skin. Big and small. Black and blue.

"They kicked me."

The tears are pouring down his cheeks.

"They broke my cars. Stomped on them."

He and Mary had got on well, through gestures here and there. Blood is thicker than water. And that is also how they understood it. Even at that age.

But it was the older children. The teenagers. They were the ones who bullied him.

He could talk to them. Or so he thought. But it wasn't what he said that had brought this upon him. But how!

They didn't want to hear his Afrikaans.

They called him *"Boer"* and hit and kicked him at every utterance.

Then he stopped talking.

It was safer that way.

"What have we done to you, my child?" a devastated Ester vomits out.

During the week I speak to Ester on the phone and she sounds like her old self again. We speak about this and that. They delivered me to Baby's on the previous Saturday and I am burning to hear about their visit the following day.

"Ma, I'll tell you when I see you."

All that I could work out was that it had gone well and that she had found peace.

On Friday afternoon she is there earlier than usual to pick me up. I update her about the family, and everything that has happened during the week, in the car on the way there. I also don't hold back about the family's misgivings about their visiting the child.

"Those are old wounds and must remain old

wounds, otherwise they will never heal," seemed to be everybody's opinion.

In my heart I know that when it comes to children, those wounds don't ever heal.

I make myself comfortable on my chair as soon as I get in and prepare myself to hear the story.

Ester leaves the room and comes back with tea. And a piece of her better-than-the-best-chocolate-cake. She always bakes it for birthdays and special occasions. Her secret is that she uses real butter and real cream and real chocolate for the icing.

My secret was half a grated potato in the mixture to keep it moist. I shared it with her. No-one would ever know from the taste.

"Now tell me, how is he doing, my child?"

And her cake melts in my mouth.

She casts her eyes down and starts telling me about the child's silence and the sores.

The taste of the butter immediately becomes rank, the chocolate bitter and the cream sour in my mouth.

"What else did you expect?" I say rattled and put my plate down.

The corners of Ester's mouth begin to shake and I become uncomfortable.

"And what did you do about it?" I ask when she tells me about the beating, as the tears cascade down her face.

Tears are the body's way of telling that it's in pain. Then they overflow.

She covers her mouth with her hand and runs up the passage.

The next moment the child bursts through the door. My heart nearly stops.

"Ouma!" he yells, as he throws himself at me.

"It was all we could do, Ma. What else?"

"Thank you, God." And I cast my eyes in the direction from which I believe all help comes. And I can't resist asking for another piece of cake.

Right there and then I have to swear on my life and on my soul going to hell that I will lie about what is happening here. You've got to do what you've got to do. Everything precious has a price.

The following week I get busy with the new wool that we'd bought the week before. The bright, almost lime-green that was on sale caught my eye and kept it.

With Annelien's help the other one was finished in a jiffy. The putting together of the blanket is the least trouble. It's also the most fun.

It is Baby who wants to know who the blanket is for.

"There isn't a little one who doesn't have one yet, Ma? Or are you crocheting for the fun of it?" she asks.

"I can't just sit still. Idleness is the root of all evil. It'll find its owner," is all that I am prepared to say, and I wrap it in a big sheet of brown paper and tie it up with string. The patterned paper is pretty but too small. And too expensive to buy two pieces.

The blanket turned out very well.

When they try and find out how it is going with the child, I say as little as possible. And stay away from lying, as much as I can.

"He is apparently doing well."

"And Ester?"

"Ask Ester yourself, if it worries you so much."

For Paul and Ester, keeping their distance from the

family turned out to be a blessing in disguise and no-one is invited over on Sunday anymore.

I am alone in the lounge and hard at work with the bright green of the new blanket. I can hear Ester busy with the pots and pans in the kitchen when Tossie, who is already looking much better, descends on me. He is so excited.

"Ouma," he almost yells.

I am busy and don't look up quickly enough for his liking.

"Ouma, look!" he says tugging at my sleeve.

"At what?"

Tossie points to his leg. And I look.

"It's much better."

"No, Ouma … look carefully!" And he's quite impatient with me.

Tossie points to a white spot on his leg where the scab's come off.

"It's looking good." What more can I say?

"Ouma, look!" And he keeps pointing at the spot. "I'm turning white!"

And I just laugh. But it isn't really funny.

I lean over the side of my chair and I pick up the big package lying next to me on the floor and I give it to him.

Without even trying to undo the knot, he rips the paper off, as children are wont to do. You just see brown paper flying.

After nearly a month nobody is any the wiser from my answers about the child. By saying that everything is going well, I haven't told a lie.

A week ago I reached the milestone of ninety. Spared

by the Lord's grace and having lived through so much.

We had tea and cake at Baby's and everyone came from far and wide. I was showered with all kinds of useless trinkets, but nothing lasting.

When my husband died, I divided all our possessions amongst the children as quickly as possible, so that there would be nothing left to fight about the day I was returned to the soil. That kind of family infighting desecrates a person's memory.

Here and there there's a photo frame and an ornament, but mostly *biltong*, dried fruit, eau de toilette and bath stuff. No more chocolates and sweets because I had announced that from now on I was on diet, otherwise they'll have to squeeze me into a coffin. And I don't want them moaning for the wrong reasons when they're carrying me.

By this time Paul and Ester are so set in their routine that no-one notices anything. They suspect something else. Paul visits in the morning and Ester in the afternoon. No-one mentions a word about the child, because now it seems as if there are other problems at home. The two of them never get seen together anymore.

But neither of them looks as if they're shedding a tear over it.

I don't get asked about it either, because by now they already know that I don't easily discuss their personal matters.

There are those who blame Paul for doing it to Ester, and others who point fingers at her for the embarrassment Paul has had to endure as a result of her unnatural love.

Ester is on the phone the following Saturday evening, and when I hear it's Baby, I tune my ears in to listen.

Paul is at a meeting, or a function or something and we expect him home much later.

"No, it's just Ma and me."

She must have asked about someone or something.

"Fine. Just busy."

It must have been Paul.

"Yes, Baby, things are going well with him too. Anyway, they were, when I last saw him," I hear her saying without missing a beat. She backs out of the entrance hall so that I can see her.

And I deduce that the conversation has turned to the child.

"No, we haven't been back. We decided it's not necessary anymore. It was probably nearly ... six weeks ago." She puts her hand over the receiver and becomes giggly. From where she's standing she can see Tossie sitting in front of the TV, wrapped up in his little blanket.

"It's a big gift, Ma," was all she ever had to say about the blanket. "You'll never know what it means to me."

I had a pretty good idea. And knew that it was worth all the effort.

"He'd grown a bit, Baby. You know how they stretch at this age." And she becomes a giggling Gerty.

"Oh, yes, I feel much better. Thanks for asking, under the circumstances."

And so she plays her game.

"He's happy. Oh, I know he's really happy. I think it's because he's with his Ouma," and she winks at me.

The next thing we see car lights reflecting against the wall of the entrance hall.

Ester puts her hand over the mouth-piece of the

phone.

"Ma," she almost screams.

The self same lights light up the curtains in the lounge. The car stops and the lights get switched off.

All I need to say is: "Tossie. Run!"

Tossie drags his blanket behind him and runs out the door. He runs past Ester, down the passage.

"I'll call you back," pants Ester, breathlessly. "Later. I think there's someone at the door."

Tossie runs straight to the wardrobe in Ester's bedroom, opens the door and climbs in. The last thing to disappear is the blanket. He closes the doors from the inside, leaving them slightly ajar.

Ester runs to the lounge window. She peeps through the curtains.

She sees that it's the Mazda.

"It's only Paul," she says, relieved.

She calls down the passage.

"It's only Sweetheart."

She turns the lock and opens the front door. Tossie runs back past her into the lounge.

"You're early tonight," she says to Paul. "You gave us a fright."

Paul remains outside. He hands her a newspaper through the bars of the security gate.

"Look!"

Ester takes the newspaper from him.

Outside he's struggling to unlock the security gate. It's one of those keys that look almost the same from both sides. I feel that in a crisis this would be a disadvantage. You can't tell what belongs on top and what below.

Ester is reading. She is dumbstruck.

Without realizing it, she emits a sound that resembles a wounded animal.

She turns around and stumbles into the lounge.

I get the fright of my life.

She begins moving around like a child who has messed in her pants. Losing control. Her whole body begins to shake.

Paul can only see her from the back and doesn't really know what's going on.

"Why are you crying? You should be happy."

Ester suddenly uncoils. She is not crying. She is laughing. She laughs and laughs uncontrollably. And she flings the newspaper into the air so that you just see pages flying.

The headlines of *The Star* reads: "*THE GROUP AREAS ACT SCRAPPED! IT IS THE END OF APARTHEID!*"

"It's the happiest day of my life!"

And she cries and cries and cries.

The scrapping of that law is a bitter pill for Paul to swallow.

At the next committee meeting, Paul has a lot to say about it again. And what Paul has to say always reaches the newspapers. Or so it seems.

The child suddenly reappears, not just at family gatherings, but also in a local rag. A man writes a letter to rap Paul over the knuckles because he'd gone so barmy about what the scrapping of *The Group Areas Act* would do to whites, and reminds him that he was a contravener of that very same law. And that he'd got away with it.

"He's back," says the article.

He then refers to Tossie as the only black child that

he's come across who calls all whites across the board "Uncle" and "Aunty" when they bump into him at the café or in the street.

I just laugh, wondering how there could be any other way? It's a very Afrikaans thing. He was brought up that way, whether you were family or not. If you have respect for someone older than you, you don't "you" or "yours" them.

"Missus" refers to the Minister's wife and "Mister" is what you call the Teacher.

But ...

Later in the year his "never in my lifetime" hits Paul smack in the face and he has to swallow his own words.

Never say never, because then you draw it to yourself.

In black and white is the proof of Paul's words. Blacks and whites don't belong at the same school desk, he had announced to the world at large.

The child is school ready and turns six this year.

From early on we could see that the child had an easy understanding of things if you explained them well to him. It always starts with a colouring-in book. Ester soon taught him how to patiently colour in within the lines. He had a natural feel for colour and didn't easily give a person purple, green or blue hair. When it came to faces, hands and feet, it was without fail the light pink colour. Never brown or black.

He could count to ten even before he had to leave. With reciting the alphabet behind him, Ester slowly but surely taught him to write letters and numbers. She has the patience of a nun with him. He scribbled on absolutely everything with wax crayons until the day he defaced Paul's newspaper, before he'd had a chance to read it. He delivered a sermon of note, because he would never lift his hand to the child.

How Paul thought that an exception would be made of Tossie is beyond me. Things had changed a lot, but not really that much.

And next year is the big step.

Or so they think.

With *Apartheid* out of the way they arrive at the nearest school and there they get a big eye-opener.

"Mister De Villiers, it's not that we've got anything against black children in the school ..." the Headmaster of the Afrikaans school around the corner from us says. "We, as the Governing Body, haven't decided yet which model we are going to follow. In principle he's more than welcome ..."

"So, what's the problem then?" Paul wants to know.

"The problem is what the parents of the other children are going to say about it," hits Paul point blank between the eyes.

By the weekend they have been through all three Afrikaans schools in the area and have also reached a dead end, even at the English Primary School, Ridge Vale Primary, which has opened its doors to black children. Paul had seen this school as the resolution.

And the resolution isn't there.

"Every time it's the same story ..." Ester says and she's angry. "All three times we have had to hear the same story of 'what-the-other-parents-will-have-to-say.' And at the English schools they have the 'his-English-isn't-good-enough-for-this-school' bullshit!" And she actually swears in front of me.

Ester realizes what she's said and she chuckles with

her hand in front of her mouth. You just hear a snort and nothing else, but the tears are streaming.

"Paul, what are we going to do?" she says when she calms down.

"Send him to the coloured school, like you said," I say.

Both she and Paul look at me as if I've completely lost the plot.

"The Father preserve us," is all she gets out. She knows the school is far away and that he'll have to go to boarding school.

"It's like having to feed him to the lions," Paul says almost biblically.

"Why, Paul?"

"Mother, he doesn't belong with them," Paul confuses me.

"Why not? They'll be able to understand him there. He speaks Afrikaans." And I give him the rope and wait for him to hang himself.

We had talked before about: If language binds people together, how come do we keep the coloureds at arm's length?

"They didn't become pale-skinned all by themselves," I told him that day. "It's the milk-in-the-coffee scenario, and now we act as if we don't even know them."

Paul changes his tune and comes forward with another story.

"You're absolutely right. But there they have sixty in a class. What sort of a chance do you think he will have then? And the standard?"

"And whose fault is that?" I throw the ball back in his court.

Like someone watching tennis, Ester looks first at me and then at him.

Then the winning ace comes from her corner.

"*Apartheid's* fault."

Now we're two against one and it helps.

"We tried with all our might to keep them dumb, Paul."

"Woodcutters and water carriers," I throw the Bible back at him.

"What would it have helped them to learn about something which they wouldn't have been able to put into practice?" Paul asks.

"Then he must become a gardener. He's almost big enough to wash a car on his own."

"And Ester can teach him to dig."

Paul is ready to burst a blood vessel.

"I don't have the energy to stand and argue with two women."

"Why not? Is this a case for men only?"

"Yes, Ma," Ester also goads him. "And look at what they landed us in?"

And Paul catches her drift.

"That's not what I meant."

"And now we sit holding the baby," Ester says, bringing us back to the problem at hand in all seriousness.

While voices are raised in heated debate all over the place about the preservation of Afrikaans, the *Springbok, Die Stem* and the flag, something happens at Paul's house that is almost inexplicable.

If the various models are standing between Tossie and going to school at the one end and only his broken

English at the other, then the solution is obvious.

At my next visit Tossie comes to greet me with a "Good Afternoon." He peeps at Paul, because he doesn't know where to next.

"How are you?" Paul prompts him.

"I know that," Tossie says with an edge to his voice. "What is 'Ouma' in English?"

"Excuse me, what did you say, young man?" Paul chastises him. "Grandmother, in her case," he prompts him.

"I'm well, thank you," I answer in Afrikaans as I turn to Paul. "What's wrong with you people?"

"We are doing it for the child. It's the only way to teach him," he answers me in English, and I can't believe my ears.

When Ester comes in with the same story, then I know it's not my imagination that's run away with me.

As she walks through the door, Tossie greets her with "Hello, Mother, how are you?"

"I'm fine, thank you for asking. And you?" she replies in polite English.

"I'm fine." And he runs out the door.

They continue in English.

"How is he progressing with his writing?" Ester asks Paul.

"I don't know. That's your department."

"By the end of the month I will be able to give him my full attention."

"What is wrong with you people?"

And they "Why?" me together.

"You can stop now. He left the room long ago."

They fling the Queen's English around, whenever the child is in sight. After everything that they have sacrificed up until now this is the last straw.

"If the schools don't want him, then we're going to give him a leg up here at home," Paul says.

Later Ester fills me in that she's resigned from work to lend a hand at home.

"He's progressing so well with writing. It's better that I teach him because, with Paul having to learn to write fast during interviews, his handwriting has become a complete scrawl."

She is still quite a way away from pension and, if she leaves before fifty-five, she stands to lose a lot.

"I must do what I must do. It's a small price to pay."

What the rest of the family has to say, I would rather not repeat. There's is whinging and whining till my ears are ringing.

Come the 17th March next year we will have to vote. A vote in a referendum where we and the blacks will have to try to make sense of what lies ahead. The statute books will then have to be rewritten to suit everyone.

Paul surmised that if the "Yes"-vote wins, it will be the last time that only whites will vote.

Never before in our history has so much money been spent to encourage people to go and make their mark on a ballot paper.

On Election Day Paul loans a wheelchair from the Old Age Home across the road to make sure that I will survive the long queues.

Usually one would keep one's vote to oneself and discuss it with nobody. With Paul it has always been: "No, no, and once more, no." Ad infinitum. In Ester's case I am almost sure of what her heart will dictate to her.

When the results are announced, the "Yes'" win with

a majority of almost 69 percent.

Here in Roodepoort the ballot papers are recounted three times, because the Conservative Party can't believe that nearly 12 000 more people have raised their voices with a "Yes."

Paul again lands in the newspapers with the belief that the newspapers, the radio and the TV have been biased all along and that it has just been false propaganda. He maintains that people have been blackmailed into voting "Yes." He refers to a bank in Braamfontein where the bank manager had told his employees the day before the election that he couldn't dictate to them how to vote, but that if the "No"-vote won, he would be forced to shut the doors of the bank the following day. According to him, Sasol had also sent out letters to their staff threatening them that if they voted "No," they would be dismissed.

It is a terrible blow to him. He had been absolutely convinced that the KP would ultimately be victorious.

With Paul like a bull with a sore thingamajig in the house, Tossie restores his pride, in a manner of means, by punching the neighbour's son with his fist because his father voted "Yes."

Poor Peter leaves the fray with a black eye.

When the last Toypom died, a month or so ago, a large dog was bought that they kept in the backyard. Everyone's nerves are shot from what is going on in the country. The townships are completely out of control.

They didn't get the big dog because they were scared. It was more because the little ones with the long hair were too much trouble, and their time and love were needed elsewhere.

Night after night we sit on the edge of our chairs, staring at the television. In the mornings I want to block my ears, because the news gets worse and worse. You never hear anything uplifting anymore. It's just carnage and killings.

The police are putting the screws on the right-wingers and the blacks are setting one another alight. Eugene Terre'Blanche falls off his horse and Paul comes back from Ventersdorp with a black eye.

Ester just laughs as she patches up her wounded knight and says it's time he grew up. He is nearly eighty.

A.P. Treurnicht, Paul's hero, dies. Even Tossie sheds a tear in empathy for Paul's loss. The poster came off the wall when Tossie had to leave. It was Ester's work and it disappeared into Paul's study.

The whites are intimidated with *"One settler, one bullet"* and they retaliate against the blacks with *"One settler, one minibus."*

Tossie is sitting at the dining room table. He's busy with his crayons.

We're watching TV because it's time for the news.

He brings his handiwork for Ester to look at and all she says is: "Eyes."

Tossie obediently puts his free hand over his eyes and turns his head away from the TV.

"It looked like a burning man, Ma."

Ester quickly changes channels, only to get the news on the other channel as well.

Tossie shows Ester his drawing and waits for her reaction.

"It's beautiful." And she smiles. "Now go and practice your writing."

Tossie goes back to the dining room somewhat deflated.

"If they can do that to each other ..." Paul says, shaking his head. "Just think what's lying in waiting for us. Now you know."

"I can't keep up. Who's murdering who?" I ask, confused.

"The Zulu's and the Xhosa's, Mother," Paul answers me.

Ester gets up and closes the curtains. For a minute she stops and stares out the window. She stares into the distance and looks as if she's deep in thought.

"Look at what Patricia got up to with Emily," comes out of the blue.

"Yes, those were Mother-in-law problems that almost led to murder," Paul cuts in.

"I was in the kitchen when I heard the screaming. It was nothing new, but this time it sounded different. Amos had already slapped Emily with a flat hand a few times before and I thought it was that time again. When Paul hauled him over the coals for hitting her, he just said that his people do that. If a woman won't listen, she must feel. She must know her place."

"I told him, if he lifts his hand to her again, I'll throw him out," Paul says vehemently.

"He never did it again. I explained to him that our people don't do that," Ester steps into the breach.

It's almost as if she's back on the plot and she can see the servant's quarters in her mind's eye.

"The next minute Amos was at the back door," she says. "He called: 'Miss Ester, Miss Ester.' When I opened the door, I saw her. Emily was covered in blood. The blood was pouring down her beautiful face. The wound in her head was gaping at me. Paul! Paul! Come and help! I screamed. I gave her a tot of brandy to help with the shock. The fruit cake that it was meant for could wait. She wasn't with the picture anymore and had already lost her understanding of this world and we had to carry her to the car. There was no time to call an ambulance. I wrapped her head in a towel and helped her and Amos into the back of the car. There was blood everywhere you looked. Paul flashed the hazard lights and we raced to Krugersdorp, because Discovery was too far. I asked Amos: What happened? 'It's my mother, Patricia. It's her.' I knew the two of them had never hit it off. She once laid into Emily with her fist, and poor Emily had come to sit with me and had cried like a baby. 'Miss, I can do nothing right in her eyes. There's always a problem. Whatever I do is wrong.' It's like that with mother-in-laws. How? I asked Amos when we were on the way. He told me that she had hit her repeatedly over the head with the heel of a shoe."

Under other circumstances it might have been funny, like in the Ben-and-Babsie (*TJ*) comic strips. There the mother also attacks everyone with a shoe or an umbrella.

"But she couldn't stop. She hit her and hit her over and over again and the whole time she kept saying: 'I told you not to marry her. I told you not to marry her.' Emily wasn't bad at all. I could vouch for that. She was my right hand. She never put a foot wrong in my house. What did she do? I wanted to scream. 'She did nothing wrong,' Amos then said. Nothing doesn't lead to near murder. 'She didn't need to do anything, Miss Ester ... She's a Zulu.'"

"When we got to the hospital we went directly to

Casualty. There they sent us from pillar to post to get her to the non-white side. There it looked like a battle-field. I at first thought that it would help if I begged as a white person for a doctor to see her. But she had to wait her turn. There were too few hands and too many casualties. Out of desperation I ran around the hospital and asked for help on the white side. There they threw the hospital rules back in my face. 'Take her to Larathong if you're in such a hurry,' the nurse on duty ordered me. 'There are just blacks there.' When she eventually got to the front, her blood was congealing. Her eyes were glassy. I thought we were going to lose her, Ma. They stitched her up and gave her pills. That's all. And kept her overnight. When we phoned the next morning to find out how she was, they told us to fetch her as they needed the bed. If it had happened today, it might have been another story. She could hide the scars under her head-scarf, but the damage went much deeper. I felt like calling the police to take Patricia away, but Paul said 'No' and told her to go. To the Transkei. Back amongst the Xhosas. Where she belonged. That was the time she left with Tossie. That's how he landed up there. And just as he started to walk properly, that's when he fell into the fire. And the wound became septic. And we had him brought back here."

When Mandela was still behind bars, he was like the martyr, Steven, in the Bible because he united all the blacks. But with him free, and the laws separating them and us abolished, old feuds rear their ugly heads again. The Zulus and the Xhosas start growling at one another. And then they bite. Bite deep until the blood flows.

"The ANC and Inkatha can't stand each other, Mother," says Paul. "They are wiping out thousands of their own kind. It's good for people to see what's going on here. Botha with his Iron Fist rule, and now De Klerk, can't sort these savages out. The one allows the other nothing."

According to Paul the best thing that De Klerk had done over the past few years was to grant freedom back to the press.

When these things were hidden from us, we slept more peacefully.

"At the end of the day we're all the same."

"Now what is that supposed to mean?" he snaps at me.

"You just have to look at what whites have done to whites in this country."

Paul frowns for a minute, thinking I'm referring to the right-wingers and the police.

"The *Boers* and the English," I help him to get there. "When it comes to power, a man will kill his own brother."

It is once again Annelien who unsettles me with her learnedness and her different outlook on life. There are two things in our history: the one we grieve over and the other that we praise ourselves for.

That the 'concentration camps' is the first one is quickly obvious to me.

"This was the first time in the world that people herded each other into camps, when men, but more so women and children, were left at the mercy of others cruelty. The rest is history. But then came the reaction against it. If you can't sort something out in a humane manner, then you need to undermine the oppressor."

She loses me for a minute because it all sounds too intellectual for me.

"What do you mean?"

"Ouma, the English were too strong for us. And to walk into the lion's den was out of the question. In the same way, we didn't stand a chance against the giant, Goliath. It was the tiny, unassuming David who had to defeat him. Not with weapons, as they were used to. But with a stone and a sling.

The fact that he lifted the sling as if aiming at a rabbit made a mockery of Goliath. He was ridiculed. Everybody thought it was the end of David. But then the stone hit its mark and the giant fell, against everybody's expectations."

I then understood that she was speaking about the rebellion.

"Yes, they didn't expect it," I say, feeling proud of our forefathers for a moment.

"Call them 'rebels;' call them 'Gideon's gang;' call them what you will; but Ouma, that was the beginning of terrorism as we now know it."

"I think you're right, my child. It's the tiny jackals that destroy the entire crop."

"We're quick to call the blacks 'terrorists,' with Mandela as the big Indoena (Chief). We say 'terrorists.' They say 'freedom fighters.' So, what's the difference?"

A feeling of displeasure comes over me, because this is not how I would want to remember the story of our own freedom.

"We've learnt nothing from our own history. The oppressed became the oppressor. That's why we live in fear today."

I want to silence her, but I don't have a defence.

"If we get too big for our own boots, the wheel begins to turn."

"Exactly, Ouma. Now the shoe's on the other foot, and it doesn't feel fitting. Doesn't suit anybody."

"We bought the shoes but we have become too big for them and now they're putting on the pressure." With my callus, I know what I'm talking about.

"Now our shoes need to be walked in before we can begin to feel comfortable again."

"Is going barefoot not an option anymore, my child?"

"No, Ouma," she says determinedly. "It's now a question of who's going to fill the shoes. And how? There's no more give and take from either side."

Tossie is finished doing what he is doing and brings me a folded piece of paper. I can't take my eyes off it.

"Thank-you, Tossie," I say in English and the tears well up.

Paul and their Englishness continue into '93. Tossie is nearly eight years old when he starts school. Ridge Vale Primary School's uniform suits him perfectly.

The Sunday before the big day he parades around for me in the full regalia. Grey shorts, white shirt, school blazer and tie. He looks too precious.

For Ester it is a day that she had never thought possible. And like any other mother she unwittingly sheds a tear.

The fact that he is so small for his age means that he doesn't stand out amongst the other children in his class. But when it comes to reading, writing and numbers, he certainly does. He is the first black child and that sets him apart. His schoolmates are white. And his friends here in the area, with the exception of Peter, are all black. Their fathers are doctors and businessmen and they didn't bring down the house prices as Paul had predicted. And when the parents of the children come to fetch and carry them, Ester serves them tea in her Royal Albert service. Paul just has to accept it. And laughs when one of their parents says to him: "It's expensive to live like the whites."

Recently the Council of Roodepoort became mixed for the first time. Paul has to take it in his stride.

Mandela brought the ten year boycott to an end, and all Paul can complain about is that people can now go to the movies and shop on a Sunday. He has to say his say.

But it doesn't happen overnight in Roodepoort. For a while it is the only place in the country where movies are not allowed on Sundays, because when the government gave the go-ahead, Roodepoort had twelve votes to ten against it.

Paul's "a principle is a principle" lands him in the papers again. In principle the Council voted against it but had to bow before Mammon and make an exception. The exception was that you could only watch movies after twelve midday. In this way it didn't interfere with the believer's salvation.

Tossie's Grade 1 report has Paul feeling as proud as any father of all the A's.

We leave at about nine on the Saturday morning. Betta has come to visit and feels like shopping. I sit in the car most of the time, because it is too much trouble to struggle in and out of the car in places where I know there is nothing for me to see or do. It is actually just nice for me to sit and watch people.

There are posters everywhere on trees, windows and

poles. I have never seen so many. For the first time in our history there are black faces. Everybody is making promises to attract voters. How many will be only the future will tell.

The big day is in two months time.

Everybody knows that this is an important date that will forever be committed to memory. But for what reason remains to be seen. How it will end up, we know even less about.

When we stop in front of Moola's, they help me out because, by now at eleven o'clock, it is boiling and inside it is always cool. The coolies pull up a chair for me so that I can sit directly under the fan. Everything is brought to me to look at. Here and there a bale of wool; a dress; and a tiny shirt that she wants me to look at and so on.

Betta becomes flustered when she wants to ask for something but doesn't know how to refer to it.

She is up and down the aisles but can't find it.

She tries to explain, but it doesn't help.

"You know," she says to Fatima, "that rough cloth. It comes in a variety of colours and it frays easily."

But poor Fatima doesn't have the vaguest idea what she is talking about, because they have so many fabrics that match her description.

Betta eventually gives up and whispers softly in her ear.

"I'm looking for 'kaffir sheeting.'"

Then Fatima knows exactly what she is looking for.

"We call it K-sheeting now. Short and sweet." And she laughs.

It has become difficult to refer to a number of things, like Kaffir-corn (*sorghum*) and the Kaffir-Wait-a-Minute tree (*Buffalo Thorn tree*).

I'm served tea. As always. Every time they ask about Tossie. They've realized by now that he's here to stay. We get all his school clothes from here.

We get home at about one o'clock and stop in front of the house.

Tossie comes out on the button, gives me a big smack on the lips, and disappears into the house with the packets.

"Afternoon Mother; Betta," Paul greets us as he comes to help me up the stairs. I'm always amazed at his patience with me.

And I am grateful.

He seats me in my chair and immediately brings me my work basket, and waits until I have taken everything out that I might need. He puts it on the floor next to me, comfortably within reach.

"Thank you, my child."

"Please excuse me, I need to spend a penny," he says, leaving the room.

"What's with the kissing," says Betta scathingly.

I'm not in the mood for her nonsense about the child and I don't even bother to answer.

It was Ester who first started the child with all the kissing. In the beginning it was hard for me. Until the day I realized: the child isn't an Adder.

"It's time for me to take you away from here, Ma, 'cause it looks to me that even you are beginning to think of him as family."

I struggle to keep quiet, but silent I will remain. Calmly I unfold the half-finished blanket, pick up the wool, and unravel a bit. I have just made the first knot when she starts up again.

"I just can't stand by and watch how you are being

subjected to these … things."

"I don't care what you think. What you think doesn't matter." I've got a good mind to rub it in, whether she likes it or not. "He makes Ester happy. And if Ester's happy, I'm happy. Do you understand me?!" I put her in her place with a filthy look and then stare her down.

And then something tells me that its time. One just knows these things. I fold the little blanket up again.

"Give me my bag."

I slowly roll up the piece of wool that I have just started with. I push the crochet hook into the ball of wool with intent. I put it on my lap, take my handbag that she's holding out to me and open it.

I put it in that day and never took it out again. I unfold the piece of paper and hold it so that she can see clearly.

Betta's mouth hangs wide open.

I eyeball her.

It's a drawing of a small black boy holding hands with a large white woman.

"Go on," I challenge her. "Read what he wrote."

She reads.

"Now read it again. This time aloud so that I can hear it coming out of your mouth that is always so full of things to say about everyone and everything."

"*Thank you, Ouma, for the most beautiful blanket,*" she reads.

"And?"

"*Love, Tossie.*"

"He is the only one of my grandchildren who made the effort to say thank you to me. Ester has brought him up well." I say it so that she knows exactly what I mean. "I hang my head in shame." I hold her gaze unrelentingly until she looks away.

I take the half finished blanket, hook and wool and put in into the needlework bag. I close it.

"Now that's enough."

That was the last time. The last time that I inflicted damage to the little bit of sight that I have left, for the sake of the children, the grandchildren, and even my great-grand-children, who have no idea how many days, weeks and months of patience and love a person puts into a task like this.

Ester has just come out of the kitchen with a heavily laden tray of sandwiches and is busy laying them out when Tossie starts up a huge racket in the passage.

"Sweetheart, Sweetheart … hurry up. I need to use the toilet!" he shouts desperately.

"Stop making such a noise," she yells down the passage to keep him quiet.

"Ma, Sweetheart is in the toilet and I need to go."

It is an old habit of Paul's to disappear into the toilet with a newspaper and to make himself at home. Maybe he needs to rest his ears from all the women in the house. Rushing him is no good because he is only over and done with his business when he gets to the back page of the paper.

"What is he doing in there?"

"Do you want to know if it's a number one or a number two, Ma?" she teases me.

"He knows its Tossie's bathroom."

"The light is better there, Ma," Ester says as she walks down the passage.

Their bathroom is further down the passage and is

dark because of the tree outside the window.

"Well, go and use our toilet. It doesn't matter either way," I hear Ester say, and Betta is about to raise her eyebrows when she sees me looking at her.

"Ah, the child can make such a fuss," she says on the way back to the dining room. "And about absolutely nothing."

Ester prepares everything and calls us to the table.

Tossie is finished and comes and plonks himself down on the chair next to Betta. He helps himself and piles up his plate.

Ester makes sure, even more than before, that the child is never short of food. Always something of everything, to be certain his meals are balanced. And on top of that she gives him vitamins to make dead sure.

Betta knows to keep her thoughts to herself, because in their house the blacks have their own plates and mugs and eat separately. It's enamel that can't be broken and is kept under the sink to make sure it doesn't get mixed up with their crockery.

Tossie knows not to start eating until Grace has been said. He waits patiently.

"What is keeping Paul? What is Paul up to?" she says, and starts calling him on the walk. "Paul. Paul. Everybody's sitting and waiting."

She knocks on the door.

"Paul. Paul?" We can hear her here in the dining room.

I didn't hear the phone ringing, but the next minute she's talking to someone and I hear her giving the address.

She comes in, white as a sheet.

"Tossie, go and eat outside on the patio so long. Say Grace before you eat, do you hear?" she says as if nothing's going on. "Excuse me."

She's on the phone again and I hear her say "Baby." And then I hear her say "Anton must come and help."

She comes back like someone who is sleepwalking.

"Ma, you mustn't go in there. I don't want you to remember him like that."

Then I know. It was his last stop.

His "Afternoon" was actually "Goodbye."

It happens like that. It's the pressure, they say. If there's a clot, it often releases just then. It shot and it hit its target.

But, for Ester, it is too unworthy of him.

He is sitting on the throne with his pants around his ankles.

She doesn't shed a tear until, with Anton's help, he is dressed and laid out on the bed.

The ambulance comes to fetch him.

Ester makes a few phone calls to let people know. The phone never stops ringing. The KP's come in their droves. Also the flowers.

By late in the evening when the stampede is over, just Ester and I remain. And the child of course. He is still too small to understand that he will never see his Sweetheart again.

Ester is busy arranging flowers in the lounge.

"Why aren't you sleeping yet?"

It is almost midnight.

"This is the last of it, Ma."

"What are you going to do?"

"I told the KP's that if they felt they should bury him, then they must bury him."

She breaks the thorns off the rose stems one by one.

"As long as the child can also come along."

She strips them of leaves. It's when the leaves hang in the water that the water goes rotten.

"All I ask is that he is buried with dignity. Surrounded by the people who really care. Not a bunch of politicians who decide on my behalf 'who,' 'where' and 'how.'"

She picks up the vase with the roses and puts it down on the coffee table next to a photo of Paul. She turns and there is sorrow written all over her face.

"This child is also my family, Ma. Whether people like it or not. He also has the right to say goodbye to Paul."

She goes to the kitchen and comes back with a tray of breakables. She starts preparing for the following day.

"Then I said to them: If he can't go into the church, then I'm not going in either. Paul would have wanted it like this. One of them was about to raise an eyebrow and I said to him: It is my duty to make sure that it is done."

This is the horse that she saddles up. And she will ride it to the bitter end.

"Then they threw the duty story back at me. My duty as a wife. Oh. I said, I will organize the refreshments and ensure that all the teaspoons lie in the same direction on the tray."

The cups are laid out and she keeps true to her word. Everything in straight rows.

"I will never raise my voice on the phone, and will serve cheese before the dessert. I will be the perfect hostess."

First the saucer, then the doily, then the cup and its spoon.

"Ma, it's as if they don't even hear me."

She interrupts herself for a moment.

"I wished the whole time that Paul was there, because he would have known exactly what to do."

"But you are now head of the house," I say, knowing full well that it doesn't work that way. "You will do what is right."

She picks up the empty tray and walks towards me.

"But I am, and always will remain, just a woman," she says, shrugging her shoulders and leaving the room.

That's when I realize: We are no different to the blacks. Yes, we can vote. They can't. But can we make a difference?

No.

We can't attend parliament. That's for the men. So what kind of say do we really have at the end of day?

None!

I was taught: You are not to talk about politics, religion or children.

If I needed something, I also had to ask my husband.

Yes, I submitted to my husband as I promised on my wedding day. Just like the blacks, I learnt well how to say: "Yes, Master. No, Master," so that our men could decide what was good for us and what not.

"Ma, they proclaim: Behind every man ..." she says when she comes back with the serviettes. "The women in our country, white and black, were always the backbone that the men needed to keep them standing upright."

She folds a serviette and slips it between the saucer and the plate.

"What's done is done."

The Sabbath comes and Ester is off to do her shopping. She's expecting the family in the afternoon and needs to be ready. There's no time to bake.

She comes back with a boot-full of packets. And a story.

I make myself useful cutting the Vienna sausages into pieces; Ester cuts the cheese into blocks; and Tossie first threads an onion, then some cheese and then the sausage onto the toothpicks. Tossie arranges the savouries that are ready around the edge of the plate.

"Now you'll need to come help me. Because now you're the man of the house," I hear her say.

Ester was busy getting cooldrinks for the children in Pick 'n Pay when she bumped into one of the APK women. The one and only Missus Swart (*Black*), she says and she is already on the verge of laughter.

"Is that not ironic in itself, Ma?"

She tells how she ducked and dived to avoid her, but feeling that she wasn't guilty of anything, pushed her trolley up to the woman.

"I looked into her trolley and she into mine. Hers was overflowing with candles, spirits and tinned food."

"'It looks like you're preparing for a party,' she jibed, 'and not for a revolution.' And she gawked at the chips and dip in my trolley."

"'Everything is sold out,' she started moaning. 'You can't get a candle or a tin of Bully Beef in any of the shops.'"

"It was on the tip of my tongue to say: It's no wonder, because the entire shop's supplies are in your trolley. What do you expect?"

"'But my husband feels: Rather too much than too

little. Look what happened in Rhodesia, Angola and Mozambique.'"

"Ma, I knew what she was getting at. The KP also sent us a list of emergency supplies which we needed to go and buy to survive the election. But I let her say her say."

"'They stole everything. The whites were even too scared to go shopping, and the little that was left became so incredibly expensive. There wasn't electricity. There was no water. Have you got a swimming pool?'"

"Yes. Why?"

"'You'll find the water purifying tablets amongst the camping stuff just next to the *braai* things,' she explained."

"What for? I asked."

"'So that you can drink it, of course.'"

"I restrained myself, because it was on the tip of my tongue to say to her: We don't pee in the swimming pool."

"'As my husband always says: Rather two months too early than one hour too late.'"

"And how do you feel about it? Because it's just my husband this and my husband that."

"'I don't get involved in man-talk. But it was when he suggested that we should barricade the windows and pile sandbags up against the outside walls, that I asked him: And who do you think is going to clean up this mess after the revolution is over? 'Do you think for one minute that we're going to have servants after they've got the vote?' he asked me. Call me spoiled, but I'm not ready for that yet. And then he said: 'You'll have to be ready. Because by that time, this house will probably belong to her!' Can you imagine that?'"

We had also seen the fax that had been doing the rounds – that a black's name was filled in next to your property. Even Paul had thought it ridiculous.

"'And you?' She wanted to know from me. 'What have you done so far?'"

"Nothing."

"'Don't say I didn't warn you.'"

"I have more important things to do than that."

"'Like what?' she asked me."

"I need to make snacks, I said quickly, because if she said revolution again, I was going to strangle her."

"'Rome's burning and you're throwing a party.'"

"As the Good Lord would have it, the next minute Tossie appeared next to me with his arms laden with Tinkies, Ma."

"Come, my child, I said unruffled. We must go and make savouries, and I looked at her. And I have a husband to bury. Good bye."

"As I was walking away I could hear her say: 'I'm sorry, I didn't know.'"

Ester goes, as with the schools, from church-to-church, and door-to-door, and everywhere it is slammed in her face.

Every time a story: "Maybe in two months time. After the election. Until then we can do what we want. Who knows what things will look like after that?"

In the meanwhile Paul has to lie on ice and wait. For nearly a week.

One of the last places on her list is a Minister from the Reformed Church. That's how far she has to spread her net.

She knocks at the manse and the door opens.

A woman stands in front of her.

"Good afternoon," says Ester. "I have an appointment with Minister Kotie MacDonald, is he here?"

"I'm Kotie," she says warmly.

"Ma, that's when I knew I'd found someone who would listen."

It was only recently that women could enter the calling. An unbelievable milestone. It started when the men got too busy to go from door-to-door month after month doing house-calls. Now it's a deaconess who reads to you from the Bible in your home, says a prayer and collects your tithes. A foot in the door, I thought. And quicker than we imagined, we were suddenly good enough for the pulpit. And there you go!

"Minister Kotie asks me about this and that, because she knows our story with the child. It is as if she can read right into my soul, without judgement."

"'You do of course realize that there are going to be a lot of people who are going to judge you for what you've done.'"

"I think for a moment she is talking about the law."

"'That you brought the child up outside of his nature,' she makes it clearer to me."

"What should we have done? Left him to his fate? What would have become of him? It was our duty as stated in the second commandment."

She agrees.

"As I am about to leave, she asks me: 'And if Paul felt that way about the blacks, why did he sacrifice so much on behalf of the child?'"

"I think to myself, Ma, that there was also the child's father, Amos. Paul was a good man. I don't think he meant any harm. He just didn't see a chance for change. I then say to the Minister: I think he did it for me."

When Ester's arrangements are finally made, the only thing left is to let Tossie's school know that he won't be there on Friday.

That is when he tells her that he doesn't want to go.

There is a moment when it looks as if all the hogwash she went through to find a church has been in vain. But for Ester, that isn't the point.

"Ma, he's too young to understand anyway. But at least the KP's now know exactly where they stand with me and how I feel."

On the day of the funeral people come from far and wide to bid farewell.

His coffin is in the front of the church, covered in the old Transvaal Vierkleur *(Four Colour)* and the Orange, White and Blue National flag.

Ester's wreath doesn't disappoint. Everything white. Roses, Lilies and Carnations.

The service ends with us singing the *Our Father*. Ester thought it suited the occasion.

Then, one after the other, the KP stand up and pay their respects. Respect for a man who felt as strongly as they do about where the blacks belong.

On the other side of the fence.

Not amongst us.

All the people present are also reminded that they must go and vote in two months time, because with *"One man. One vote,"* we are really in the minority. And if they are to get a two thirds majority, they will undoubtedly chase us into the sea.

Paul's remains don't find rest with the rest of the family. He had made arrangements for himself and Ester in the overfull Roodepoort Cemetery. It is reserved for people who have lived in this vicinity for more than twenty years.

We could also have come under consideration, but our arrangements had worked out differently. The plots were cheaper in Roodepoort-West and there was enough place for the whole family.

We ended up amongst the blacks and he in a place surrounded by the whitest of the whites. As he would have wanted it.

It's Election Day and the ANC victory comes over Paul's dead body. He had always said that.

The queues are kilometres long and the black people wait patiently to make their marks for the first time.

With me in the wheelchair, we are ushered to the front with: "Go to the front with the Old Missus."

Silence comes before the storm, or so we were taught. But when the storm that everybody anticipated and feared should have come, we were met by a deafening silence instead.

It is months later, when she is busy packing up Paul's life, that she finds the letter. His resignation from the KP.

He'd never posted it.

She never hears from the KP again. There is an occasion or two when the Nationalists pop in.

It isn't only in her ears that the KP become silent. After the election one hears little about them and the AWB.

And Tossie ...?

Paul would have been so proud of him. He achieves honorary colours, not only in sport, but also for his academics.

Today he speaks Afrikaans and English fluently. And Zulu, Emily's language, and Xhosa, like his father.

Emily is still in and out of Sterkfontein. We hear almost nothing about her anymore. When she does get out, she stays with Evelina.

And Amos ...?

Amos died in 1997. He burnt to death in a kaia *(shack)*. He was drunk. They say he fell asleep with a cigarette in his hand.

Although Ester offered, Tossie didn't want to go to his funeral either.

When Tossie wants to join a soccer club and needs proof of his birth date, Ester discovers that his birth had never been registered.

Tossie wants her to register him as De Villiers.

It would be so easy.

But Ester doesn't want to.

All that she has is a piece of paper that Amos had written on: Raymond Vuyo Xele. Such a proud name. And the date: 4 April 1985.

That's when the picture becomes clear to me.

You see. It was never hate. Love and hate go hand in hand, if you look at it like that. Two sides of the same coin.

It's prejudice that that slams your heart shut like a door caught in a draft.

And prejudice comes from ignorance. Because something that you don't understand, you don't know how to love.

With prejudice comes fear.

If a person could just look back early enough and wonder: What kind of danger did the Roman Catholic Terror and the Red Terror hold for me, personally, at the end of the day?

All the quivering and quaking. And what for?

The same applies to the terror of the Blacks.

It was fear.

We were made to fear them.

Fear is the thing that holds love at arm's length.

And to overcome this fear, you need to learn to love the very thing that you are so afraid of.

If you don't know the nature of a shark, you think that they are all out there waiting to devour you. So you'd rather not venture into the water.

Ester stood on the bank. Then she was knocked in. And she had to quickly learn to tread water to stay afloat. It was then that she realized how easy it is to swim.

And strangely enough, there are still those who say: One day that *kaffertjie* is going to slit her throat.

CPSIA information can be obtained at www.ICGtesting.com
Printed in the USA
BVOW08s1419061016

464352BV00001B/4/P